JOURNEYING WITH GOD

THOUGHTS TO INSPIRE AND ENCOURAGE

PASTOR'S PEN
SERIES

Pastor's Pen Series
Samuel "Sam" McCook

© Hope Fellowship Press 2017

All rights reserved. No part of this publication may be reproduced, distributed, or transmitted in any form or by any means, including photocopying, recording, or other electronic or mechanical methods, without the prior written permission of the publisher, except in the case of brief quotations embodied in critical reviews and certain other noncommercial uses permitted by copyright law.

First Published, 2017

ISBN 978 –976 –95997-0-3

Publishing Manager and Managing Editor: Glynis E.N. Salmon
Copy Editors: Faith McCook and Carmen Patterson
Cover and Page Design: Omar Dillion

Contact Us:
Hope Fellowship Press
Hope Fellowship Church
23 Molynes Road
Kingston 10
Jamaica
Email: hfsministries@gmail.com
Telephone: (876) 906-8013; (876)505-6063
Sale and Ordering Information:
Sale: Books are available for sale at Hope Fellowship Church and Leading Bookstores in Jamaica
Orders: Contact Hope Fellowship Press at hfsministries@gmail.com, or at the address and/or telephone numbers above
Special Discounts: Applied to quantity purchases by Churches, Organizations, Associations, Libraries, Bookshops, Individuals

DEDICATION

Not unto us, O Lord, not unto us, but to Your name give glory, because of Your mercy, because of Your truth.-
Psalm 115: 1

This book is dedicated to the honour and glory of God, in whose service I journey through life, seeking always to walk closely with him, truly knowing his voice and in all things be obedient to his will.

ACKNOWLEDGEMENT

The Hope Fellowship Church Family and wider Christian Community, who join me as brothers and sisters on this journey of service to the Lord, and whose desire is to worship him in spirit and in truth, has inspired the sharing of the thoughts documented by the **"Pastor's Pen."** Thank you for your "journeying mercies".

The unwavering love, support, counsel and encouragement of my wife Faith 'Betty' who helped me to keep the Pastor in the Pastor's Pens, our children Sean and Stephanie, brothers, Dale, Oral, Wayne, and Robert, sister, Ann-Marie, whose journey ended too soon and Beverley, our 'big', little sister; the vast extended family and friends, who have all served to both challenge and nurture my faith and kept me "on purpose."

I acknowledge the strong foundation of faith and trust in God, that my parents Leslie and Selma laid for me, through their lives of sacrificial service and dedication to God and his people. They loved God completely, loved us unconditionally and inspired us continually.

I thank God for *Hope Fellowship Press*, and the Ministry that facilitated the production of this publication. I extend sincere appreciation to the "journey companions" of Publisher and Managing Editor, Glynis Salmon, who put heart and soul into making this book a reality; and Omar Dillon, graphic designer, for the contribution of his tremendous gifts and talents.

Thank you to all who have invested in the acquisition and promotion of this book. May you be inspired and encouraged in *your Journey with God, knowing that you can live your calling . . . by the Power of God, for the glory of God.*

CONTENTS

"...who testified to your love before the church. You will do well to send them on their journey in a manner worthy of God." - 3 John 1:6

Dedication	i
Acknowledgement	ii
Foreword	vi

CHAPTER 1
Direct My Path O Lord

Greetings And Salutations	2
The Blank Page	4
'Tis God's Hands That Leadeth Me	6

CHAPTER 2
Lead Me And I Will Follow

Go Forward!	10
Keep Going	12
Reaching Your Rehoboth	14

CHAPTER 3
Be Of Good Courage

U-Turn On The Emmaus Road	18
Press On!	21
No Giant Too Big For God (And You)	23

CHAPTER 4
In You O Lord I Put My Trust

It's A Marathon	27
Go For The Mountain!	30
That Second Wind	33

CHAPTER 5
He Is My Shield And Defender

In The War Zone	37
Our Secret Weapon	39
Calm And Contented	41

CHAPTER 6
Pray Without Ceasing

A Time To Fast	45
Plodding And Praying	47
Pray And Do	49

CHAPTER 7
Living Change God's Way

The Journey Of Transformation	54
Embracing Change	56
Pathway To Transformation	58

CHAPTER 8
Whatever State I Am In, I Am Content

Solutions Wear Out, But God Does Not	63
By The Rivers Of Babylon	65
No Visa Required	68

CHAPTER 9
God's Way, All The Way

Babylon By Faith	72
Fireproof Faith	75
The Love That Will Not Let You Go	77

CHAPTER 10
Stand Firm In The Faith

The Steadfast Love Of The Lord Never Ceases	82
A Forgiving God For A Forgetting People	84
Delivered From Distress	86

CHAPTER 11
Abiding In The Shadow Of The Almighty

A Higher Calling	90
Alive In Christ	92
Shaken But Not Stirred	94

CHAPTER 12
Overcoming Through Communion With God

Honestly God . . . This Is How I Feel	98
From Conflict To Communion	100
Let The Beauty Of Jesus Be Seen!	103

CHAPTER 13
Hope For Today, Strength For Tomorrow

The Compassion Of Christ	109
Will You Be Made Whole?	111
Where He Is There Is Hope	114

CHAPTER 14
. . . Fallen, But We Will Rise Again

Lord, It Was Me	118
"Failing Forward"	121
Inner Strength	123

CHAPTER 15
Bearing Witness Along The Way . . .

Do You Put Pigs First?	127
Called To Be Salt And Light	130
Learning To Listen	132

CHAPTER 16
Lift Up Our Children and Families

Children First	136
Family For Better	139
Our Children, In His Hands	142

CHAPTER 17
A Promise Forever: Honour Thy Mother and Father

The Special Gift Of Mothers	146
Good, Good Father	149
"Abba" Father	152

CHAPTER 18
Behold The Lord God

Good News! Great Joy!	156
Joy Beyond Christmas	159
The Present Of Presence	161

CHAPTER 19
I Know That My Redeemer Lives

Life Amazing!	169
Wisdom In Our Wilderness	171
Something Special About him	173
He's Standing In The Ring With You	175

CHAPTER 20
The Parable of the Prodigal Son

The Illusion Of Independence	180
Maximize The Moment	182
Free To Choose	184

CHAPTER 21
Increase The Fruits Of Your Righteousness

Honour God's Harvest With Our Best	188
Giving From 'Borrowed Goods.'	190
The Rhythm Of The Seasons Of Life	193

CHAPTER 22
Scripture Has A Power That's Undeniable

Gems Of Truth	197
Hidden Treasure	199
Extravagant Worship	201

CHAPTER 23
Time, Timing, God's Direction And Authority

The Value Of Time With God In It	205
God's Time Is All The Time	207

CHAPTER 24
His Grace Is Sufficient

Grace And Peace From Our Risen Lord	211
Grace And Peace	213
Grace And Peace In Abundance	215

CHAPTER 25
Exalted As Head Over All

Our God Reigns	219
Our God Of Salvation	222
Stand Up Stand Up For Jesus	225

CHAPTER 26
We Give You Thanks, O Lord God Almighty

God Is Always Good	229
Give Thanks	231
Give Thanks With A Grateful Heart	233

FOREWORD

"Let your eyes look directly ahead and let your gaze be fixed straight in front of you. Watch the path of your feet and all your ways will be established. Do not turn to the right nor to the left; Turn your foot from evil" - Proverbs 4:25-27

The **Pastor's Pen** was really for me a casual chat with a small community of persons that I knew, cared about, and with whom I had a lot in common. It was the congregation at *Hope Fellowship Church* that I served for many years as a Lay Leader, and was now serving as Pastor. I could write honestly and freely about the thoughts I had, the experiences affecting me and views on issues I cared about.

I wrote in the context of my Faith. A Faith shaped very much by my early years growing up in the small farming community of Caledonia in Westmoreland, the first of seven children of Leslie and Selma McCook. They were Pastors and we lived in the 'Parsonage' a few yards from the church building. It was an eclectic setting. . . Daddy preaching deeply researched and profound Sermons to a congregation that enjoyed the high points and endured the lows; the Hymns and Sankeys; Choir presentations and "Singspiration" Choruses; 'lively' testimonies; tambourines and organ, saints and sinners. . .

It is a Faith that struggled with the complex interplay of religion and science, of Eurocentric Christianity and American Missionaries in a world of Bob Marley, Black Power, and the New World Order; of sincere Christians and charismatic charlatans; of a loving, gracious God and an evil painful world; of resilient faith and lurking doubt. It is a Faith that rests in the known and knowable, that refuses to allow the unknown and unknowable to displace or diminish it. It is a faith that makes the journey of life possible, cushioning the pain and enabling the joy.

The **Pastor's Pen** is not heavy theology or robust doctrine. I am not competent to attempt either. It is simply a collection of thoughts and insights from a fellow "traveler" on the journey of life. One who continues to be amazed at the providence of God, and the precious privilege of His presence in the ordinariness of life.

It is my prayer that this book will encourage you in your own journey of life, to embrace and enjoy the presence of God who wants to walk with you, over your hills and valleys, your sunny days and stormy nights and when the walking gets too hard, and the road gets too rough, He is there to lift you up and carry you on. With Him you will never walk alone. Walk good my friend.

God bless
Pastor Sam

DIRECT MY PATH O LORD

Psalm 25: 4-5 Make me know Your ways, O LORD; Teach me Your paths. Lead me in Your truth and teach me, For You are the God of my salvation; For You I wait all the day.

James 1:5 But if any of you lacks wisdom, let him ask of God, who gives to all generously and without reproach, and it will be given to him.

Psalm 27:11 LORD, lead me in Your righteousness because of my foes; Make Your way straight before me.

Psalm 61:1-2 For You are my rock and my fortress; For Your name's sake You will lead me and guide me.

Psalm 43:3 Let me hear Your loving kindness in the morning; For I trust in You; Teach me the way in which I should walk; For to You I lift up my soul.

Psalm 16:7-8 Send out Your light and Your truth, let them lead me; Let them bring me to Your holy hill And to Your dwelling places.

John 10:3-4 Make me walk in the path of Your commandments, For I delight in it.

Proverbs 3:5-6 To him the doorkeeper opens, and the sheep hear his voice, and he calls his own sheep by name and leads them out. When he puts forth all his own, he goes ahead of them, and the sheep follow him because they know his voice.

2 Chronicles 6:26-27 Trust in the LORD with all your heart And do not lean on your own understanding. In all your ways acknowledge Him, And He will make your paths straight.

Isaiah 57:15 Search me, O God, and know my heart; Try me and know my anxious thoughts; And see if there be any hurtful way in me, And lead me in the everlasting way.

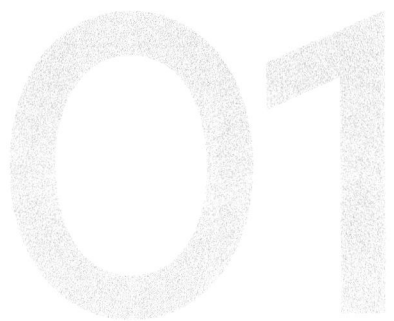

When I came to the spring today, I said, 'LORD, God of my master Abraham, if you will, please grant success to the journey on which I have come."
- Genesis 24:42 NIV

GREETINGS AND SALUTATIONS

THE BLANK PAGE

'TIS GOD'S HANDS THAT LEADETH ME

GREETINGS AND SALUTATIONS

The Apostle Paul is regarded as one of the greatest Christians who ever lived. He started out as one of the strongest and most aggressive opponents of the gospel, but he had a miraculous encounter with Christ, and it changed his life forever. He was an extremely gifted servant of Christ who was instrumental in spreading the Gospel and establishing communities of faith that have become the Church of today.

One of the most significant contributions of the Apostle Paul however, was as one of the inspired writers of the Bible. His letters, found in the New Testament, were written to individuals and churches providing guidance, knowledge and encouragement, at a time when there was much confusion, conflict and challenges in the relatively young movement of Christians.

His letters grappled with very difficult issues and situations. His tone, in some of the letters, was well moderated and reasoned; in others, strident and almost aggressive; and in some, gentle and persuasive. However, one cannot read his letters and not be struck by the graciousness of his salutations.

In his salutation, in the letter to the Romans, he establishes his credentials as an apostle and emphasizes his mission and his message. He gives the story of Christ and his work of redemption in a few words and then connects that message to the readers. His greetings to the Romans comes with a freshness and conviction, that is uplifting to the spirit, thousands of years later. Let us take it as our own and allow it to simmer in our souls.

" The Good News was promised long ago by God through his prophets, as written in the Holy Scriptures. It is about his Son, our Lord Jesus Christ . . . Through him God gave me the privilege of being an apostle for the sake of Christ, in order to lead people of all nations to believe and obey. This also includes you who are in Rome (Hope) whom God has called to belong to Jesus Christ. And so I write to all of you in Rome (Hope) whom God loves and has called to be his own people: May God our Father and the Lord Jesus Christ give you GRACE AND PEACE." - Romans 1:6-7 (TEV)

THE BLANK PAGE

A blank page can be an inviting and appealing opportunity to express one's thoughts and ideas. It can also be an intimidating and challenging reminder of work to be done, words to be created and ideas to be formulated in ways that can be appreciated and helpful to others. Writing the Pastor's Pen is a mixture of both and sometimes more of one than the other.

There are times when writing is easy, words flow fluently and some would say exquisitely on to the blank page, ideas back up like cars at a gas station during a gas strike and words come alive, rich in color and texture. At other times words tumble clumsily on to the blank page, struggling for rhyme and rhythm, ideas are scarce and words are dull and grey.

But writing is a discipline, we write not only when the 'juices are flowing' and words and ideas come easily, we also write when it would be easier to do something more relaxing, anything else but write. We write because there is something worth saying, something that may be of value to only one person for whom the words that others find inelegant and dull, may be just the word 'in season.'

The future is a lot like the blank page in front of a writer. Filled with potential and promise. The canvas for the artist's masterpiece and the vehicle for expressing the best of our humanity. Sometimes it fills us with dread and anxiety, at other times it fills us with excitement and anticipation. But like the writer, we are affected by our emotions, but we do not have to be controlled by them.

We can decide what words we put on the page, what ideas we choose to express, what impact we desire to make, what experiences we wish to create. We can use bold, colorful and vibrant words that brighten the page and explode with joy. Or we can use words that are sober, reflective and even sad, words that come from deep and sensitive places not easily shared with those outside, yet when expressed, connect with and console others going through their own time of difficulty.

And so we keep writing, filling one blank page after another as our book of life is compiled. The pages of joy and laughter, the pages of sadness and tears, the pages of confidence and certainty and the pages of confusion and doubt as they become the pages of our lives, the story of our days. And as we write we remind ourselves of the master writer, the one who journeys with us every moment of the day, the one whose presence and guidance will ensure that at the end of our story, the final line will be . . . well done.

"Therefore we also, since we are surrounded by so great a cloud of witnesses, let us lay aside every weight, and the sin which so easily ensnares us, and let us run with endurance the race that is set before us. Looking unto Jesus, the author and finisher of our faith..."
- Hebrews 12:1-2 (NKJV)

'TIS GOD'S HANDS THAT LEADETH ME

Sometimes when I sit to write the **Pastor's Pen**, I have a clear sense of what I am going to say and the words flow easily and naturally. However there are times when it is neither easy nor natural, ideas and thoughts swirl around in my head, but none readily stick. I keep asking, is this thought helpful ? Is it relevant? Is it realistic? Is there someone who needs to hear this? Or am I just speaking to the wind.

In those times I realize my own dependence on God and my need for His guidance and His inspiration. I ask Him to take my thoughts and my craft and mold them into an instrument that gives hope to someone who is discouraged, clarity to someone who is confused, faith to someone who is struggling with doubt, and new life to someone who is slowly dying inside.

There is always the temptation to find nice sounding scriptures, soothing thoughts, inspiring verses and hope that they will inspire and encourage. But sometimes they are not what is needed, sometimes they are like an overdose of syrup, too sweet to drink and impossible to swallow.

We live in difficult times, testing times. Someone describes our world as a hurting place with hurting people. As Christians we are not insulated from the hardships, the pain and the hurts. It is foolish to walk with our heads in the clouds and ignore the pressures and the pain around us, and in us. The path of the Christian is a path of pain. Jesus our Lord was described as a *'man of sorrow and acquainted with grief.'* We speak admiringly of the Early Church, of the Apostles, of Peter and Paul, but they paid dearly for their faith.

There was something however, about how they faced the difficulties of their lives. They had a robust and resilient faith, a faith that was focused more on enduring and overcoming, than on avoiding. A faith that was focused more on faithfulness than on favor.

We were told that "in the last days perilous times will come.... men's hearts will fail them for fear." These are the last days. We need "last day's faith". Fighting faith. Faith that faces the future with confidence. Confidence that the God who took the early church through its trials and testings, will take us as twenty first century Christians through our own challenges, and land us safely and victoriously on the other side..

Let us encourage each other with the words of the hymn, He leadeth me, oh precious thought, oh words with heavenly comfort fraught, what ere I do, where ere I be, still 'tis God's hands that leadeth me.

Remember what Paul wrote during a time of severe testing; " Being confident of this, that he who began a good work in you will carry it on to completion until the day of Christ." - Phil. 1:6 (NIV)

LEAD ME AND I WILL FOLLOW

Psalms 25:5 *Lead me in your truth and teach me, for you are the God of my salvation; for you I wait all the day long.*

Psalms 32:8 *I will instruct you and teach you in the way you should go; I will counsel you with my eye upon you.*

Psalms 37:23-24 *The steps of a man are established by the Lord, when he delights in his way; though he fall, he shall not be cast headlong, for the Lord upholds his hand.*

Proverbs 3:5-6 *Trust in the Lord with all your heart, and do not lean on your own understanding. In all your ways acknowledge him, and he will make straight your paths.*

Jeremiah 1:7-8 *But the Lord said to me, "Do not say, 'I am only a youth'; for to all to whom I send you, you shall go, and whatever I command you, you shall speak. Do not be afraid of them, for I am with you to deliver you, declares the Lord."*

James 1:5-8 *If any of you lacks wisdom, let him ask God, who gives generously to all without reproach, and it will be given him. But let him ask in faith, with no doubting, for the one who doubts is like a wave of the sea that is driven and tossed by the wind. For that person must not suppose that he will receive anything from the Lord; he is a double-minded man, unstable in all his ways.*

Proverbs 11:14 *Where there is no guidance, a people falls, but in an abundance of counselors there is safety.*

1 John 4:1 *Beloved, do not believe every spirit, but test the spirits to see whether they are from God, for many false prophets have gone out into the world.*

Isaiah 30:19-22 *For a people shall dwell in Zion, in Jerusalem; you shall weep no more. He will surely be gracious to you at the sound of your cry. As soon as he hears it, he answers you. 20 And though the Lord give you the bread of adversity and the water of affliction, yet your Teacher will not hide himself anymore, but your eyes shall see your Teacher. 21 And your ears shall hear a word behind you, saying, "This is the way, walk in it," when you turn to the right or when you turn to the left. 22 Then you will defile your carved idols overlaid with silver and your gold-plated metal images. You will scatter them as unclean things. You will say to them, "Be gone!"*

1 Corinthians 1:25 *For the foolishness of God is wiser than men, and the weakness of God is stronger than men.*

"Then they said, Ask God whether or not our journey will be successful. Go in peace, the Priest replied. For the LORD is watching over your journey." - Judges 18:5-6

GO FORWARD!

KEEP GOING

REACHING YOUR REHOBOTH

GO FORWARD!

Many of us have given up on making resolutions because we have seen so many of them quickly fade into the land of forgetfulness, never to be remembered anymore. But setting goals can be a very useful exercise. Goals give us something to aim for, lends focus to our lives and helps us to navigate the twists and turns of life. Goals are important for us as individuals, but they are also important for us as families, and as a church.

Our goal as individuals and as a Christian church community, is to grow. We want to thrive, grow and flourish spiritually. Maturing and demonstrating the transforming love of Christ. We want to see the numbers of persons attending, and becoming members of church grow, as we under the leadership of the Holy Spirit, create an environment of worship that lifts up Christ and draws men and women to him. We want to see our impact and influence as Christians grow, as we become true neighbors to those around us, demonstrating in practical and meaningful ways, the compassionate love of Christ.

Growing can be difficult, uncomfortable, costly and even painful and because of this, many times we resist growth.

We prefer the ease and comfort of the old ways, the familiarity and convenience of the known. We shy away from the challenges and risks of going forward. But to live like this is not to live, but to exist. It is to rob ourselves of the richness and vibrancy of life as God intended it to be lived. It is to live like the despised 'one - talent' man, who buried his talent and with it, the hope and promise of the better future that would have been his.

I invite you to get onboard the 'growth train'. Experiencing God's miracles and myriad blessings in our lives as individuals and as a community. A Journey through which we are going to experience tremendous spiritual growth as we surrender ourselves to the leading of the Holy Spirit. A journey through which we will claim new territory for the King and discover the liberating power of losing ourselves and finding it in Him. An exciting life awaits, let us not waste time looking back, but let us go forward.

As Joshua took over the leadership of the Children of Israel, he faced overwhelming challenges. The mighty Jordan river stood between him and the promised land, and awaiting him in the promised land were fierce enemies, seasoned warriors, giant-like men who "dwarfed" his inexperienced and wilderness-worn stragglers. But Joshua was not intimidated because he knew he had God on his side.

We have God on our side. With God on our side, we are confident that even though the waters may be rising and the enemies are armed and dangerous, we will go forward, because as God was with Joshua, so will He be with us. "Have I not commanded you? Be strong and courageous. Do not be afraid; do not be discouraged, for the LORD your God will be with you wherever you go." - Joshua 1:9 (NIV)

KEEP GOING

The birth of the early Church was a remarkable demonstration of the power of God to transform lives. Moved and empowered by the Holy Spirit, a small group of people who were not particularly distinguished or outstanding in any way, had captured the attention of the entire city.

Their main spokesperson was a fisherman who looked, behaved and spoke like one. Their message was different. Some said their message was not only different, but strange. Others said "weird" even. They spoke about a man who had been executed a few weeks before on a hill reserved for society's rejects. They claimed that he was no ordinary man. They claimed that he was the Son of God. Their message was that he could forgive sins and make people's lives new.

Their message was accompanied with unusual activities . . . people were being healed of various diseases, demon-possessed people were being delivered and signs and wonders were common. Many people responded to the message and became followers of Christ, the Church grew rapidly and the changes in people's lives was amazing.

There were those who felt that this manifestation would eventually slow down, fade away and become a part of folk history. Others actively opposed it and used every available means, including persecution and even killings, to stop its progress. But the Church not only survived, it thrived.

Many reasons may be given for the resilience of the Church then. The powerful evidences of God's presence, the workings of the Holy Spirit and the leadership of the Apostles certainly played important parts. But there is a theme of perseverance and commitment that is inescapable when one reads about the life of the Church in the Book of Acts, and these seem to have been an essential part of this resilience.

The Believers kept trusting God, kept serving Him, kept going, regardless of the circumstance. They knew that the race was not for the swift, but for those who would persevere to the end. Commitment, consistency and continuing, are essential elements in being effective Followers of Christ. Without them, there can be no sustained change in our individual lives, or in the life of the church. Without them, there can be no transformation.

On this journey, our enthusiasm for change, our gifts and abilities, our intentions and actions, must be combined with diligence and faithfulness. Yes, there will be 'transformational moments,' times of exceptional accomplishments and successes, but there will also be times of slow, or no progress at all. Times of reversals and setbacks. Times when things are unexciting and the journey becomes a drudgery. Those are the times when our true Christian quality and character is revealed. The times that separate the true believers from the pretenders and the "called" from the crowd. Times that call for continuing. Times to keep going. Let us develop the discipline of 'continuing' and discovering its transforming power. Let us keep going!

"And, they continuing daily with one accord in the temple, and breaking bread from house to house, did eat their meat with gladness and singleness of heart, Praising God, and having favor with all the people. And the Lord added to the church daily such as should be saved." - Acts 2:46-47 (KJV)

REACHING YOUR REHOBOTH.

"He moved on from there and dug another well, and no one quarreled over it. He named it REHOBOTH, saying, now the Lord has given us room and we will flourish in the land." - Genesis 26:22 (NIV)

Water is an essential commodity. "Water is life", it is said. When we experience severe drought in our land, we are all relieved when it ends and plants begin to grow green and flourish with new life, and water flows fresh and clear. In the Middle East where much of the land is dry and desert-like, water is of great importance and is highly valued. So too it was in the time of Isaac. Water was of great importance for domestic, economic and strategic reasons. Wells were therefore a critical asset.

Even though Isaac was by then quite wealthy and had much livestock, without access to a reliable and secure source of water, he would lose his livestock, his wealth, possibly his family and ultimately his life. Every time he dug a well however, it caused strife with his neighbors who claimed priority rights to the wells and made life miserable for him.

In spite of the challenges, Isaac did not stop. He continued to dig more wells until he dug a well that did not attract strife and he named it Rehoboth, his 'God given space'. A space free from the quarrelsome influences of the herdsmen of Gerar. Having found his space, he declared that he would now flourish in the land.

He had to give up wells his father had dug before him. He had to give up wells that he had discovered himself. He had to give up some things that were his by right, but he gained something more valuable and lasting, he gained his Rehoboth, his 'God given place' of peace and prosperity.

I pray that each of us will find our Rehoboth. Our place above the war and strife, where the clamoring for water and the scramble for personal space and advantage, are left behind with the herdsmen of Gerar. A place where we will find peace and flourish. A place where God will visit us and say as he did to Isaac: " Do not be afraid, for I am with you; I will bless you . . . for the sake of my servant Abraham."

BE OF GOOD COURAGE

Deuteronomy 31: 6 *Be strong and courageous, do not be afraid or tremble at them, for the LORD your God is the one who goes with you He will not fail you or forsake you*

Proverbs 3:26 *For the LORD will be your confidence And will keep your foot from being caught.*

Proverbs 3:5-6 *Trust in the LORD with all your heart And do not lean on your own understanding. In all your ways acknowledge Him, And He will make your paths straight.*

Romans 8:28 *And we know that God causes all things to work together for good to those who love God, to those who are called according to His purpose.*

Joshua 1:9 *Have I not commanded you? Be strong and courageous! Do not tremble or be dismayed, for the LORD your God is with you wherever you go*

Isaiah 41:10 *Do not fear, for I am with you; Do not anxiously look about you, for I am your God I will strengthen you, surely I will help you, Surely I will uphold you with My righteous right hand.'*

1 Corinthians 15:58 *Therefore, my beloved brethren, be steadfast, immovable, always abounding in the work of the Lord, knowing that your toil is not in vain in the Lord.*

Psalm 27:1 *The LORD is my light and my salvation; Whom shall I fear? The LORD is the defense of my life; Whom shall I dread?*

Numbers 14:8-9 *If the LORD is pleased with us, then He will bring us into this land and give it to us--a land which flows with milk and honey. "Only do not rebel against the LORD; and do not fear the people of the land, for they will be our prey. Their protection has been removed from them, and the LORD is with us; do not fear them.*

Joshua 1:7 *Only be strong and very courageous; be careful to do according to all the law which Moses My servant commanded you; do not turn from it to the right or to the left, so that you may have success wherever you go.*

"Do not fear, for I am with you; do not be afraid, for I am your God. I will strengthen you; I will help you; I will hold on to you with my righteous right hand." - Isaiah 41:10

U-TURN ON THE EMMAUS ROAD

PRESS ON!

NO GIANT TOO BIG

U-TURN ON THE EMMAUS ROAD

"But we were hoping that it was He who was going to redeem Israel."-

The two disciples of Jesus were walking away from Jerusalem, they were on the road to Emmaus. They tried to encourage each other as they walked. They were probably exchanging thoughts about what they would now do with their lives following the death of Jesus.

They had many questions and few answers. The confidence and certainty that they had built up during their time with Jesus, was gone. The comradeship and sense of belonging that they had been accustomed to when Jesus was around, no longer existed. They were all like lost sheep.

Peter who was always upbeat, always on the move, always ready to fight for the cause and defend their Lord, was missing in action. He was keeping a low profile. After his stout declarations of loyalty to Jesus, he buckled under pressure, disowning him and denying him. The last time he was seen, he was weeping bitterly, ashamed of himself and broken in spirit at failing the one whom he had sworn to defend.

The rest of the crew was hardly better. Many had gone back to their old lives and old ways. There was nothing holding them together, there was nothing to fight for, nothing to hope for. Jesus had been killed and with his death, all their hopes and dreams had died. Their faith and belief in the new kingdom he talked about, had died with his death.

This journey to Emmaus was not a walk of faith. It was a journey of despair, discouragement and doubt. It was a journey away from the other disciples, away from the brethren, away from Jerusalem, away from their faith. They had turned their backs on Jesus, because as far as they knew, he had died and that was the end of the story.

Unknown to them Jesus was also on the Emmaus road. His journey was not one of doubt or discouragement however, but a journey of redemption. He was there to answer their questions, remove their doubts, replace their despair and restore their faith. He was there to change their story and to change their lives. He was there to change their destination and their disposition. He was there to assure them that he may have been killed, he may have died, but he was very much alive.

Sometimes we find ourselves on our own Emmaus road. We may have experienced some great loss,
set-back or disappointment. Our faith seemed incapable of delivering solutions when it mattered. We feel like our community of faith was not holding together and the "Peters" in our lives can't help, because they are dealing with their own loss and pain.

But Jesus knows our heart, he hears the questions that we ask and he feels the despair we are experiencing. He is on our Emmaus road, with his message of faith and hope. He wants to engage us in a destination-changing and life-transforming conversation. He wants us to experience the 'burning of our hearts' that will lift our spirit and restore our faith. Let him join you on the walk and let him speak life into your being.

"So it was, while they conversed and reasoned, that Jesus Himself drew near and went with them... Now it came to pass, as He sat at the table with them, that He took bread, blessed and broke it, and gave it to them. Then their eyes were opened and they knew Him: and He vanished from their sight. And they said to one another, did not our hearts burn within us while He talked with us on the road, and while He opened the Scriptures to us? So they rose up that very hour and returned to Jerusalem.." - St Luke 24: 15 – 33 (NKJV)

PRESS ON!

"Press along saints, Press along, in God's own way."

I was listening to an interview with a noted Author recently, and he spoke about the temptation to give up in the middle of a project because of the overwhelming pressures that one sometimes faces. He described this phase as the *'messy middle.'*

He went on to describe how as the deadline for completing one of his books drew closer, and the amount of writing still to be done seemed impossible, he felt like returning the advance to the Publisher, and abandoning the project altogether. However, he persevered and completed the book. He missed the deadline by several weeks, but the book became a *New York Times Bestseller* and propelled him to much greater success.

I can identify with his feelings, as I am sure you can too. We invest significant time and resources into an undertaking and then somewhere in the middle, when we think things should be easier, we face stormy seas and serious setbacks, we are stuck in the *'messy middle.'* But it is in these situations that we have to exercise the power of *pressing*.

The *Apostle Paul* understood the challenges of the 'messy middle' and encourages us to forget the things of the past and to press on. You may be in the 'messy middle' of an important project, a job, a relationship, a course of study, school, or you may be in what you regard as the 'messy middle' of your life. Whatever *messy middle* you are in, now is not the time to give up, now is the time to press.

Paul gives us some advice in effective pressing. He says that we should forget the things that are behind. In other words, let go of the past, focus on the task at hand and keep the prize in view. *Pressing* is not purposeless. We expect to achieve something worthwhile at the end of the process. That is why we started in the first place.

So like Paul, let us keep aiming for the prize and when the pressures of the 'messy middle' seem overwhelming, don't give up, just press harder, press smarter and enlist God as your pressing partner. With Him by your side, nothing can stop your progress.

"I want to know Christ and the power of his resurrection and the fellowship of sharing in his sufferings, becoming like him in his death, and so, somehow, to attain to the resurrection from the dead. Not that I have already attained all this, or have already been made perfect, but I press on, to take hold of that for which Christ Jesus took hold of me. Brothers I do not consider myself yet to have taken hold of it. But one thing I do. Forgetting what is behind and straining towards what is ahead, I press on toward the goal to win the prize for which god has called me...." - Philippians 3:10-14 (NIV)

NO GIANT TOO BIG FOR GOD (AND YOU)

Canaan was the land of promise, a place reserved for God's chosen people, the children of Israel. It was a fertile and prosperous land, a land that flowed with milk and honey. A land with established cities, villages, farms and infrastructure. It is what would be described today as a 'turn-key' option. There would be no need for them to start from scratch. Most of what would have been required to establish settlements and communities, had already been done.

There was however a 'catch'. A major challenge in their way. The land was occupied. It was occupied by giants as the spies described them. According to the spies, compared to these giants, the Israelites were like grasshoppers. Although their description was exaggerated, it was essentially true. The land was occupied by people who were far more equipped and experienced than these former slaves.

The Children of Israel were far from prepared to challenge these people. A realistic assessment of the situation would conclude that they were no match for the opposition. After living in slavery for centuries, traveling through the Wilderness for forty years, constantly on the move and dealing with crisis after crisis, it is reasonable to expect that after this, they would much prefer a long vacation, a quiet retreat or a comfortable retirement home.

But the land, even though promised to them, would not be handed to them on a platter. They would have to fight to acquire it, and they would have to fight to keep it. The Wilderness was God's place of preparation for them, it was their University. It was where they would learn the skills required to conquer and keep the land.

But the lessons were not about military strategy, guerrilla warfare, special ops, or any of the subjects one would think essential to the battles they would face. Rather the lesson was really about learning to hear God, understand God and to follow God. He was their secret weapon, he was their 'nuclear option.'

God wanted them to know, that so long as they were marching under his banner, there were no giants too big, no army too strong, or no enemy too clever for them to overcome. He would be their God and they would be His people. In the Wilderness he demonstrated that this was no empty statement but a powerful reality.

In Leviticus he details his expectations of them and reaffirmed his promises to them. He tells them: " I the Lord your God brought you out of Egypt so that you would no longer be slaves. I broke the power that held you down, and I let you walk with your head held high." - Lev. 26: 13 (TEV)

IN YOU O LORD I PUT MY TRUST

Luke 1:37 Therefore, since we are surrounded by such a great cloud of witnesses, let us throw off everytshing that hinders and the sin that so easily entangles. And let us run with perseverance the race marked out for us.

Jeremiah 17:7-8 But blessed is the one who trusts in the Lord, whose confidence is in him. They will be like a tree planted by the water, that sends out its roots by the stream. It does not fear when heat comes; its leaves are always green. It has no worries in a year of drought and never fails to bear fruit.

Proverbs 3:5-6 Trust in the Lord with all your heart and lean not on your own understanding; in all your ways submit to him, and he will make your paths straight.

Proverbs 16:3 Commit to the Lord whatever you do, and he will establish your plans.

Isaiah 43:2 When you pass through the waters, I will be with you; and when you pass through the rivers, they will not sweep over you. When you walk through the fire, you will not be burned; the flames will not set you ablaze.

Psalm 143:8 Let the morning bring me word of your unfailing love, for I have put my trust in you. Show me the way I should go, for to you I entrust my life.

Psalm 121:3 He will not let your foot slip, he who watches over you will not slumber.

Psalm 62:7 My salvation and my honor depend on God; he is my mighty rock, my refuge.

Proverbs 29:25 Fear of man will prove to be a snare, but whoever trusts in the Lord is kept safe.

Psalm 91:1-2 Whoever dwells in the shelter of the Most High will rest in the shadow of the Almighty. I will say of the Lord, "He is my refuge and my fortress, my God, in whom I trust."

04

"Trust in the Lord with all your heart, and do not rely on your own understanding. Acknowledge him in all your ways, and he will make your paths straight" - Proverbs 3:5–6

IT'S A MARATHON

GO FOR THE MOUNTAIN!

THAT SECOND WIND . . . AND THIRD

IT'S A MARATHON

Jamaica is famous for its sprinters, and by any standard of measurement, rank among the top sprinting nations in the history of the sport. When it comes to long distance running however, Jamaica does not feature at all, as this is a field dominated by African runners from nations like Kenya and Ethiopia.

The sprints are exciting and dramatic races, there is no room for error. A bad start is almost certain to result in a losing finish. In these races, seconds matter, and they are over before you know it. Marathons are different. They are relatively slow and strategically paced. There is no bursting out of the blocks. They take hours and many people regard them as monotonous and boring and often lose interest in the progress.

Of the two types of races however, the one that most parallels life, is the marathon. Marathons are run on all kinds of surfaces, in all kinds of weather, over a distance of 26.2 miles. It requires exhaustive preparation, careful diets, mental toughness and physical endurance.

We are all running in the marathon of life. In this race we are not given a trial run. We have one shot at the race, we cannot defer, delay or decline. The starter's gun went off the moment we took our first breath.

The first few miles may be easy, but the course gets progressively harder . . . steeper hills, deeper valleys, rougher surfaces, more distractions and difficulties . . . sometimes we wish the race was easier. We may even look enviously at others who just seem to be gliding effortlessly along, whilst we are struggling just to make the next stride. But something remarkable is happening as we move forward. . . our muscles are being built up, we are developing our rhythm, we are becoming stronger, our breathing is becoming easier and we are discovering an energy and endurance that we never thought we had.

Today we are each in the process of another mile in our marathon of life. It is a mile mixed with times of joy and satisfaction as we conquered our hills and overcame our valleys, times of quiet endurance as we moved forward slowly but steadily on stretches of the course that appeared unfamiliar and strange. But there may have also been times of discouragement and pain. When taking the next step required more than we could muster. When we wilted in the heat and stumbled under the pressure.

Let us remember that life is not a sprint, but a marathon. That the race is not for the swift, but for the runners that keep going and going and going. . . runners that make it to the finish line, even if they have to crawl across.

The Apostle Paul completed his marathon and gives us great encouragement along our journey . . . *"But we have this treasure in jars of clay to show that this all-surpassing power is from God and not from us. We are hard pressed on every side, but not crushed, perplexed but not in despair, persecuted but not abandoned, struck down but not destroyed. We always carry around in our body the death of Jesus, so that the life of Jesus may also be revealed in our body…… Therefore we do not lose heart. Though outwardly we are wasting away, yet inwardly we are being renewed, day by day."* - 2 Corinthians 4:7-16 (NIV)

GO FOR THE MOUNTAIN!

Mountains are very important features of the natural landscape. If the world had no mountains the landscape would be boring and monotonous. Mountains bring character and drama to the terrain.

But mountains have value beyond the beauty they lend to the horizon. Mountains influence climate, agriculture, health, lifestyle, security and many other aspects of human existence. Mountains are generally viewed in a positive light, and are widely regarded as sources of blessing. We sometimes describe great spiritual moments as 'mountain top' experiences.

But sometimes mountains have negative effects, and the word "mountain" may be used to describe insurmountable odds and overwhelming obstacles. It is therefore quite easy to be discouraged, when we face the 'rough side of the mountain.'

The story of Caleb 'the mountain man', has inspired many people over the centuries. He was among the twelve spies sent by Moses to spy out the land of Canaan. All twelve reported back on how good the land was, but the majority, ten of them, strongly advised against going there, because of the giants they would have to contend with. Caleb and Joshua however, were not intimidated by the giants and encouraged Moses and the people to go and take the land.

Many years later, when they entered the land, and the time came to give each tribe their portion of the land, Caleb made a bold request. He asked for the mountain. He was eighty-five years old at the time and was by any definition, a senior citizen. He had been to the land before, and had seen the giants for himself. He knew that the mountain he selected was occupied by the Anakites, fierce giants. But still he chose the mountain.

For Caleb, Hebron was his mountain of promise, a beautiful place, fertile and well-fruited, with commanding views of the low lands below. But there was a problem, a huge problem. For him to properly take possession of the land, he would have to drive out the giants, he would have to go to war. But this did not discourage him, he was going to take on the mountain, and the giants would have to go. This mountain of promise, was also a mountain of problems, big problems, but Caleb overcame the problems, and lived to enjoy the promise.

We all have mountains of promise in our lives, but we may be held back by fear of the problems associated with the promise. The problem may be our age . . . old like Caleb or young like Timothy; or it may be opposition . . . in the form of giants that make us look like dwarfs. Each of us has our unique set of problems, but we should not allow them to keep us from getting to live on our mountain of promise.

The God who took eighty-five-year-old Caleb to the top of the mountain, is waiting to walk with you, to work with you, to go to war for you, to work with you, to climb your mountain with you. He wants to be there with you, when you stand on the peak of your mountain and look out on where you have been, and say with a heart of worship, "look what the Lord has done!"

"Now the men of Judah approached Joshua at Gilgal, and Caleb son of Jephunneh the Kenizzite said to him.... Now then just as the Lord promised, he has kept me alive for forty-five years since the time he said this to Moses, while Israel moved about in the desert. So here I am today, eighty-five years old! I am still as strong today as the day Moses sent me out; I'm just as vigorous to go out to battle now as I was then. Now give me this hill country (mountain) that the Lord promised me that day. You yourself heard then that the Anakites were there and their cities were large and fortified, but, the Lord helping me, I will drive them out just as he said." - Joshua 14: 6-12 (NIV)

THAT SECOND WIND...
AND THIRD

From time to time, we need a second wind to get us moving. Elijah was one of the persons who needed a second wind. He was one of the last persons one would expect to get 'stuck', but he did.

After all, Elijah was the "poster boy" of prophetic power. He did not only have the gift of prophesying, but through him, God had done phenomenal things and he had become a legend in his own time. His gifts were accompanied by a passion and a zeal that was all consuming. Elijah was the kind of prophet no one messed with (ask the prophets of Baal), he was the real deal.

We see him at the peak of his game on Mount Carmel. The entire nation, led by King Ahab, had rejected Jehovah as God and had adopted foreign gods, chief of which was Baal. On Mount Carmel, Elijah engaged the prophet and followers of Baal in a "do or die" competition. Elijah's God triumphed over Baal and Elijah stood vindicated and triumphant.

But it was not just the fact of victory that was impressive, it was the way he did it... with drama and bravado. He did not just win, he demolished the opposition. This was certainly a time for celebration. A time to savour the moment. To acknowledge that his faith in God was not misplaced. Inexplicably it would seem however, we find Elijah, instead of being triumphant, afraid and fleeing from Jezebel.

If we had a chance to speak with Elijah, we would probably show him all the reasons why he should not be afraid. We would list his victories and remind him that he had been through far worse situations before and emerged victorious through God's grace. We would tell him to 'get a grip' of himself. But Elijah was so low in spirit, that it is unlikely that any of our encouragement and affirmations would have had any uplifting effect on him.

But God was with Elijah, and took him on a journey of self-discovery and renewal. He showed him that there was important work to be done and that he was the one to do it. God turned his situation around. He renewed him and redirected him. He took him from fearfully fleeing from Jezebel, to flying in a fiery chariot. He took a depressed and suicidal prophet who was drowning in self-pity, and got him going again.

Elijah went on to complete his mission in life, he did not allow his state of fear and weakness, or the lows in his life to define him, or to determine his destiny. He allowed God's strength to be made perfect in his weakness, faithfully carrying the treasure in his broken vessel. His story is used in the New Testament to encourage us and remind us that he: "was a man with a nature like ours, and he prayed earnestly that it would not rain; and it did not rain on the land for three years and six months. And he prayed again, and the heaven gave rain, and the earth produced its fruit." - James 5:17-18 (NKJV)

HE IS MY SHIELD AND DEFENDER

2 Timothy 1:7 - For God hath not given us the spirit of fear; but of power, and of love, and of a sound mind.

Hebrews 13:6 - So that we may boldly say, The Lord is my helper, and I will not fear what man shall do unto me.

Joshua 1:9 - Have not I commanded thee? Be strong and of a good courage; be not afraid, neither be thou dismayed: for the LORD thy God [is] with thee whithersoever thou goest.

Psalms 27:3 - Though an host should encamp against me, my heart shall not fear: though war should rise against me, in this will I be confident.

1 John 4:18 - There is no fear in love; but perfect love casteth out fear: because fear hath torment. He that feareth is not made perfect in love.

Matthew 6:34 - Take therefore no thought for the morrow: for the morrow shall take thought for the things of itself. Sufficient unto the day is the evil thereof.

Hebrews 10:35-36 Therefore, do not throw away your confidence, which has a great reward. For you have need of endurance, so that when you have done the will of God, you may receive what was promised.

Matthew 6:34 Therefore do not worry about tomorrow, for tomorrow will worry about itself. Each day has enough trouble of its own

Hebrews 4:16 So let us come boldly to the throne of our gracious God. There we will receive his mercy, and we will find grace to help us when we need it most

James 1:12 God blesses those who patiently endure testing and temptation. Afterward they will receive the crown of life that God has promised to those who love him.

05

"Consider it a great joy, my brothers, whenever you experience various trials, knowing that the testing of your faith produces endurance. But endurance must do its complete work, so that you may be mature and complete, lacking nothing." James 1:2-4

IN THE WAR ZONE

OUR SECRET WEAPON

CALM AND CONTENTED

IN THE WAR ZONE

Beloved, the whole truth, and nothing but the truth, is that following Christ is not for the faint - hearted.
Salvation is not a retirement plan. It is not an escape route from the challenges of life on earth. It is no accident that the cross is one of the most recognized symbols in Christianity. As followers of Christ we are expected to be 'cross carriers.' We are required to take up our cross and follow him.

This is why Peter could use this peculiar turn of phrase in 1 Peter 4:12, " Beloved, think it not strange concerning the fiery trial which is to try you, as though some strange thing happened unto you." He is telling us not to be surprised when 'fiery trials' come our way, don't get bewildered and confused, don't throw our hands up in the air as if something weird is happening, it is not weird, it is not strange, it is the way of the believer.

When soldiers encounter 'fiery attacks' from the enemy, they don't look quizzically at each other and ask, why are we being fired at? They expect it. That is what war is about. They were trained to 'think it not strange' when the enemy shoots at them, that is what enemies do.

We have a huge enemy. We are engaged in a great war, the war of the ages. Our enemy is smart, experienced, focused and will use any weapon in his attack. But he is not invincible. His side has already lost the war. Our General is invincible. He has already declared victory as he stands with his fighters. He is our shield and buckler.

So think it not strange, that you are experiencing "fiery attacks" from the enemy. These "attacks" may inflict pain, they may create problems, they may inspire fear, but they will not destroy you, for greater is he that is in you, than they that are fighting against you. We do not fight in our own strength, we do not fight with carnal weapons, our lord fights for us, he has never Lost a battle before and he is not going to start losing today.

Let us continue to pray and support each other. We are stronger together with the love and power of God that binds us. The Apostle Peter knew what it was to be in the fight, and God has used him to speak to us today, and to encourage us as we take our place in the 'battle of the ages.' He advises us: *"Wherefore let them that suffer according to the will of God, commit the keeping of their souls to him in well doing, as unto a faithful creator."* - 1 Peter 4:19 (JKV)

OUR SECRET WEAPON

" O what peace we often forfeit, O what needless pain we bear, all because we do not carry, everything to God in prayer. . ."

In old - time western movies, the hero would stand tall with huge pistols on his hips, ready to outgun any challenger. Many times, however, the battle was not won by the big guns, but by a small gun cleverly hidden away in some unexpected secret place, that takes the opponent by surprise. The secret weapon then becomes the game changer.

As Christians, our "secret weapon" is prayer. Not just 'ordinary' prayer, but the prayer that flows from the Holy Spirit that resides in us. This idea is powerfully expressed in the book of Romans, where Paul the Apostle recognizes our weaknesses and limitations in our "big guns" of prayer, and exposes the secret ammunition concealed in our prayer. He says that, "we do not know how to pray, but the Spirit Himself intercedes for us with groanings too deep for words."

The Spirit enters into our pain and crisis, and takes it upon himself, feeling it, carrying it and relaying it, in a manner more profound than words, beyond utterance or expression. When we pray, we give the Spirit room to operate, space to occupy, permission to act as our advocate, to speak up for us. In fervent prayer, the Holy Spirit "goes to battle" for us.

As we take our position, standing tall with the power of faith in our heart and prayer on our lips, and fearlessly face our opponent , we can be assured that whether we are facing the most vicious challenge, the most complicated approach, or the trickiest "draw", God is ready to be our defender and dispatch the enemy. We subject ourselves to unnecessary worry and anxiety because we try to fight our battles all by ourselves. "

"In the same way, the Spirit also helps our weakness; for we do not know how to pray as we should, but the Spirit Himself intercedes for us with groanings too deep for words. And He who searches the hearts knows what the mind of the Spirit is, because He intercedes for the saints according to the will of God. And we know that God causes all things to work together for good to those who love God, to those who are called according to His purpose." - Romans 8:26-28 (NASB)

CALM AND CONTENTED

One of my favorite statements in the Bible is: "I have learned in whatsoever state I am therewith to be content". It is a statement that can be easily misconstrued as promoting idleness, lack of ambition and carelessness. But these words came from one of the busiest men of his time, a man who was a leading thinker and author, a man who walked with the mighty and the weak, the rich and the poor, the saint and the sinner, the Apostle Paul.

He was passionately committed to serving Christ and to spreading the gospel throughout the then known world. It was a cause for which he had sacrificed many things and endured great suffering. In fact, these words were written on one of his many stays in prison. He was no arm-chair Theologian. Neither was he some writer sitting in a tranquil place, crafting nice-sounding words. His words are those of a seasoned warrior who had fought many battles, faced many foes and had his faith severely tested in many ways. His body beaten, bruised and broken, but his spirit intact, vibrant and alive.

He presents himself to us as an example of the transforming power of the gospel of Christ. He is challenging us to find contentment where we are, in whom we are, with what we have and with the God who resides in us. He is challenging us to avoid the entanglements of the world that if given room, can easily stifle us and rob us of our life.

He is not calling us to 'drop out' of the world, to lay down arms, or to ignore the realities of our lives. He is instead inviting us to place a premium on contentment; to discover for ourselves, that 'godliness with contentment is great gain.'

The secret to Paul's contentment, is found not in where he was, or in what was happening to him. It is found in his growing realization of the power of Christ. The certainty that nothing he would face would be too much to handle. In one passage he describes them as 'light afflictions.'

Paul's experience was uniquely his, just as your experiences and mine are unique to us, but each of us has the same key to contentment. That key is a growing faith and trust in God . . . that we belong to Him, that he is with us and that he is working all things for our good. Contentment is found in letting him do the driving and learning to enjoy the ride.

I pray that these words, written by someone whose faith in God was tested more than most people, will strengthen us as we confidently face our many challenges and opportunities.

"Not that I speak from want, for I have learned to be content in whatever circumstances I am in. I know how to get along with humble means, and I also know how to live in prosperity; in any and every circumstance I have learned the secret of being filled and going hungry, both of having abundance and suffering need. I can do all things through him who strengthens me . . . and my God shall supply all your needs according to his riches in glory in Christ Jesus . . . the grace of the lord Jesus Christ be with your spirit." - Philippians 4:11-23 (NASB)

PRAY WITHOUT CEASING

1 Thessalonians 5:16-18 Do not be anxious about anything, but in every situation, by prayer and petition, with thanksgiving, present your requests to God. And the peace of God, which transcends all understanding, will guard your hearts and your minds in Christ Jesus.

Matthew 18:20 Let us then approach God's throne of grace with confidence, so that we may receive mercy and find grace to help us in our time of need.

Romans 12:12 And when you pray, do not keep on babbling like pagans, for they think they will be heard because of their many words.

Hebrews 4:16 But when you pray, go into your room, close the door and pray to your Father, who is unseen. Then your Father, who sees what is done in secret, will reward you.

Colossians 4:2 Therefore I tell you, whatever you ask for in prayer, believe that you have received it, and it will be yours.

Psalm 18:6 But when you ask, you must believe and not doubt, because the one who doubts is like a wave of the sea, blown and tossed by the wind.

1 John 5:15 But to you who are listening I say: Love your enemies, do good to those who hate you, bless those who curse you, pray for those who mistreat you.

James 1:6 Therefore confess your sins to each other and pray for each other so that you may be healed. The prayer of a righteous person is powerful and effective.

Jeremiah 29:12 Be joyful in hope, patient in affliction, faithful in prayer.

1 John 5:14 Devote yourselves to prayer, being watchful and thankful.

"Then I proclaimed a fast there, at the river Ahava, that we might humble ourselves before our God, to seek from him a safe journey for ourselves, our children, and all our goods." - Ezra 8:21

A TIME TO FAST

PLODDING AND PRAYING

PRAY AND DO

A TIME TO FAST

Our daily routine easily crowds God out of our lives. We are busy with the legitimate activities of making a living, earning our honest bread, taking care of our children, putting food on the table, keeping a roof over our heads, clothes on our backs and money "under the mattress". Many of us barely have time to catch our breath, we are so busy working, working, working. As we rush about making life, our relationship with God gets pushed further and further into the background.

Yes, we go to church, we live moral lives, we do the things good Christians do, but do we love God? Do we enjoy God? Do we look forward to spending time with Him? Christianity is all about our relationship with God, about experiencing His love and being consumed with a burning desire to return that love. The Pharisees did all the right religious things, but they lacked this passionate love for God, and were harshly described as 'white washed sepulchers.'

When we embark on sacrificial journey of Fasting, we deprive ourselves of food for varying lengths of time to focus on God and seek a closer walk with Him. This journey of fasting can be a 'breakthrough fast' for you and for me. A breakthrough in our relationship with God that ignites our passion for Him, that will lead us to take Him from the back room of our lives, and place him at the centre of it.

A breakthrough that will so convince us of His presence and His power, that we will replace our worry and our anxious approach to life, with a quiet and confident trust in Him for everything. A breakthrough in our relationships, that will enable us through the love He 'sheds abroad in our lives' to love others and live as true neighbors. A breakthrough in the negative circumstances of our lives, that will free us to become all that He wants us to be.

Fasting is less about what we do, and more about who we are doing it with, Jesus Christ our Lord and Savior. He is our partner in this Fast. Let us embrace Him, and walk closely with Him. Let us on this journey discover how much He loves us, and wants us to experience the abundant life that he provides.

Remember, He taught us to pray: " Our Father who is in heaven, Hallowed be Your name. Your Kingdom come, your will be done, on earth as it is in heaven. Give us this day, our daily bread, and forgive us our trespasses, as we forgive those who trespass against us; And lead us not into temptation, but deliver us from evil; for Yours is the Kingdom, the power and the glory , forever and ever, Amen! - Matthew 6: 9-11 (NASB)

PLODDING AND PRAYING

For many of us as Christians, our walk with God has become a slow and painful plodding. We can barely put one spiritual foot in front of the next. We have lost the spiritual spring in our steps, the fire is there, but it is barely flickering. The joy is there, but it is buried so deep, that our faces have forgotten.

One may say, what a depressing scene, what a discouraging assessment, what a hopeless condition. But I beg to differ, I believe that it is when we have come to the end of our rope, when we have exhausted our own options, when our own streams of joy have dried up and our own self-righteousness is exposed for the filthy garment that it is, that we are ready to acknowledge our desperate need for God and begin to 'pant for him like the deer.' "They that hunger and thirst after righteousness, shall be filled."

We approach Him therefore with Fasting and Prayer, as empty and broken children, gathering at the feet of our Father, to have him place his healing hand upon us, to wrap us in his redemptive embrace and to cover us in his unfailing love. "Lord, we wait for you with open arms, and empty hearts, fill us till we overflow."

"Even now . . . declares the Lord, return to me with all your heart, with fasting and weeping and mourning . . . I will repay you for the years the locusts have eaten, the great locust and the young locust, the other locusts and the locust swarm, my great army that I sent among you. You will have plenty to eat until you are full, and you will praise the Lord your God, who has worked wonders for you; never again will my people be shamed. Then you will know that I am in Israel, that I am the Lord thy God, and that there is no other; never again will my people be shamed." - (Excerpts from Joel 2)

PRAY AND DO

One evening a young lady boarded a bus to make her way home after a hard day's work. She expected that it would be an uneventful, maybe even monotonous journey and that she would soon be home to relax and recover from the rigours of the day. Unknown to her however, that would be her last journey. On that bus, on her way home, a group of cold-blooded killers shot her to death at point blank range.

Her death sent shock waves through the society, a society that has witnessed more than its fair share of violence and murder, a society that has become 'used' to the killings and desensitized by the number of murders recorded each year. But there was something about the killing of this young lady that touched the society's collective nerves.

It could be the callousness of the act, the fact that she was a young 'trying' person, the fact that she was a police and had chosen a line of work that required her to place her life at risk in order to protect us; or it could be, the brazenness of shooting someone in front of so many witnesses; or the simple fact that another precious life has been recklessly and cruelly taken away by the gun.

Whatever the reason, there was understandably, a great outpouring of grief and expressions of support for her family and for the police. But after the rush of grief and the gush of tears, the nagging questions remained loud and persistent, demanding answers . . . How did we get to this place as a society? What can we do to reduce violent crime and murder in our land?

It is well established that the level of violence that many societies are now experiencing is due in large measure to social disorder, particularly in families. Too many persons are content to talk about the crisis and make criticisms, but are not willing to join forces and take their part in doing something towards facilitating positive change.

Each of us has a role to play, as individuals and as groups. It starts with choosing to become a part of the solution and not acting as if it does not concern us, or that it is bigger than us. We do not need to wait until crime and violence is at our doorsteps, to respond. Let us all, and as Christians especially, be among the doers, whether what we do is small or large, significant or insignificant, noticed or unnoticed, let us do what we can whilst we can, with God's help.

We can start by praying. Praying and Fasting. Some may reject this as old fashioned, escapist and mindless. However, as Christians we believe in the Living God, who hears and answers prayers. He promises to heal our land when we humble ourselves, pray and turn from our wicked ways. Prayer must be our first response, but it should not be our only response Let us continue to pray to our Father and Defender that we will live in a more peaceful society , and that our children will inherit the blessings of citizens living righteousness.

The words of the National Anthem of Jamaica, which is really a Prayer in song, holds true for Jamaica and nations across the

world, and reads in part:
Eternal Father Bless our Land
Guard us with Thy mighty hand
Keep us free from evil powers
Be our light in countless hours . . .

LIVING CHANGE GOD'S WAY

Romans 12:2 *Do not be conformed to this world, but be transformed by the renewal of your mind, that by testing you may discern what is the will of God, what is good and acceptable and perfect.*

2 Corinthians 5:17 *Therefore, if anyone is in Christ, he is a new creation. The old has passed away; behold, the new has come.*

2 Corinthians 3:18 *And we all, with unveiled face, beholding the glory of the Lord, are being transformed into the same image from one degree of glory to another. For this comes from the Lord who is the Spirit.*

Psalm 51:10-12 *Create in me a clean heart, O God, and renew a right spirit within me. Cast me not away from your presence, and take not your Holy Spirit from me. Restore to me the joy of your salvation, and uphold me with a willing spirit.*

Galatians 5:19-26 *Now the works of the flesh are evident: sexual immorality, impurity, sensuality, idolatry, sorcery, enmity, strife, jealousy, fits of anger, rivalries, dissensions, divisions, envy, drunkenness, orgies, and things like these. I warn you, as I warned you before, that those who do such things will not inherit the kingdom of God. But the fruit of the Spirit is love, joy, peace, patience, kindness, goodness, faithfulness, gentleness, self-control; against such things there is no law. ...*

James 1:22-25 *But be doers of the word, and not hearers only, deceiving yourselves. For if anyone is a hearer of the word and not a doer, he is like a man who looks intently at his natural face in a mirror. For he looks at himself and goes away and at once forgets what he was like. But the one who looks into the perfect law, the law of liberty, and perseveres, being no hearer who forgets but a doer who acts, he will be blessed in his doing.*

"I am sure of this, that He who started a good work in you will carry it on to completion until the day of Christ Jesus" Philippians 1:6

THE JOURNEY OF TRANSFORMATION

EMBRACING CHANGE

PATHWAY TO TRANSFORMATION

THE JOURNEY OF TRANSFORMATION

Life is really about change. There is no progress without change. All around us we see change. Growth requires and results in change. The seed germinates and becomes a plant. The plant grows, gaining height and keeps reaching to the sun. It produces leaves. Some produce blossoms which change into fruits that are reaped and eventually consumed. But the story does not end there. The change continues and the journey of the next crop begins, and so it continues cyclically, year after year.

This journey of transformation is about change. It is about becoming better. It is about rejecting the notion that we are stuck in the present, that we are incapable of changing, that the negative aspects of our being and our lives are fixed for life. The message of Jesus is a message of change. It is a rejection of things as they are, and an embracing of things as God wants them to be.

He declared that He did not come to save the righteous, that those who are whole do not need a physician. His message is for the broken and the sick. Broken in body, in spirit and in mind. Those whose lives are broken, those whose souls are empty, those for whom hope is gone. He declares to this "broken world" in which we live, and to us in our brokenness that; " I am the resurrection and the life."

The woman at the well, whose life and being was consumed with a desperate, but futile search for love and fulfillment, met Christ and her life was changed forever. She could not contain her joy. The freedom from her tarnished past, the discovery of brand new possibilities, the discovery of her true worth, and the experience of love that had eluded her in the past, caused her to run and excitedly declare; "come see a man who told me all that I did, is not this the Christ?"

The process of personal transformation involves an exploration of ways in which we can each, with God's help, experience a greater sense of well-being and mastery in our lives.

I invite you to take this journey of transformation. A journey in which God not only provides the road- map in his Words, but provides a companion and guide in the person of His Holy Spirit. I invite you in the words of the Psalmist, to taste and see that the Lord is good.

"I appeal to you therefore, brothers, by the mercies of God, to present your bodies as a living sacrifice, holy and acceptable to God, which is your spiritual worship. Do not be conformed to this world, but be transformed by the renewal of your mind, that by testing you may discern what is the will of God, what is good and acceptable and perfect. For by the grace given to me I say to everyone among you not to think of himself more highly than he ought to think, but to think with sober judgment, each according to the measure of faith that God has assigned. For as in one body we have many members, and the members do not all have the same function, so we, though many, are one body in Christ, and individually members one of another" - Romans 12:1-21 ESV

EMBRACING CHANGE

Life in the twenty-first century is filled with rapid changes. Many of these changes have made life easier, more comfortable, more exciting and interesting. We are able to go faster, do more, know more and accomplish more. Knowledge and access to knowledge has increased beyond anyone's imagination.

These changes have had many positive effects on society and has resulted in great improvements to the quality of life of people around the world. But the changes have also had negative effects, in some cases disastrous effects. Many advances in technology have been hijacked by people with evil intent and are being used to corrupt the minds and behaviors of young and old alike. In other cases, vast criminal enterprises have used the advances being made, to expand their reach, resulting in untold suffering, pain and death.

This rapidly changing environment is creating high levels of uncertainty and anxiety in society. The traditional structures and systems of society are having great difficulty coping with the pressure of these changes, and the cracks are beginning to show. Institutions such as the family, the church and the school, are all experiencing varying degrees of unrest and turbulence.

People are wondering what is happening to the world, what is happening to them? How do they cope and adjust in these challenging times? Some people look for escape in religious traditions that do the thinking for them, and blindly follow the instructions of some guru, or charismatic leader. Others retreat to 'the country', or create some place where they can lead a "simpler" life. Others 'go with the flow' and hope that they will be spared the negative aspects of the times. Many are embracing the changes however, and are seeking to find effective ways of coping and thriving in this 'new world.' As Christians this ought to be our approach.

Change is inevitable and necessary. As Christians, we are the products of change and we are going to remain in the change mode until we see Christ and become like Him. Change should not surprise, or shock us. Our faith is designed for changing times, it equips us to live in unfavorable and even hostile environments. Jesus recognized the times in which his followers would live, in Matthew 24 he gives a graphic description of the worsening condition of the world and the challenges it would present to the faithful. But he prayed that they be not ' taken out of the world but that they would be kept from the evil of the world.'

When he commissioned his followers to go into all the world, he gave them the assurance of his presence. We can appropriate that promise today, in this changing and challenging world in which we live, we can face the future with faith, knowing that, "He will not leave us nor forsake us." Hebrews 15:5 (KJV")

"Finally, be strong in the Lord and in the strength of his might. Put on the whole armor of God, that you may be able to stand against the schemes of the devil. For we do not wrestle against flesh and blood, but against the rulers, against the authorities, against the cosmic powers over this present darkness, against the spiritual forces of evil in the heavenly places. Therefore take up the whole armor of God, that you may be able to withstand in the evil day, and having done all, to stand firm" - Ephesians 6:10-13

PATHWAY TO TRANSFORMATION

The journey of transformation has impacted each of us in different ways. For some of us, the process has clarified issues in our lives, provided new ways of looking at old problems, pointed us in new directions in our search for 'life solutions' and given us new tools to cope with life.

The process of transformation is less about our becoming better for the sake of being better, but it is more about becoming better so that we will make a greater contribution to those around us, and the world in which we live. Our value as human beings should be measured not by how much we consume, but by how much we contribute.

Jesus Christ is a perfect example of how a transformed person lives. He lived with purpose and was clear about his mission. He cared about people and extended himself to ease their pain. He maintained healthy relationships, keeping a small circle of close friends with whom he spent time and shared companionship.

He had a busy life, speaking to huge crowds, healing many persons, providing comfort and hope to others, feeding thousands and dealing with a host of challenges and opposition. But he knew when to leave the pressing demands of ministry and spend time in prayer and solitude. He did all this with an apparent calmness and confidence that indicated that he knew who he was.

He was willing to stand up for what he believed, even if it made him unpopular, or exposed him to danger and even death. He was passionate about his cause and his cleansing of the Temple, showed that he was a man of action. He had the capacity to be gentle and caring. His blessing of the children contrasted with the insensitivity and coarseness of his Disciples.

The Gospels are filled with stories that illustrate how Jesus lived and reports what he said. From the accounts of the Gospels, we can piece together a clear model of how a transformed life looks. But Jesus is not only our model for transformation, he provides the means for our transformation.

Through his death and resurrection, he provides for each of us, a pathway to transformation. A pathway that is available to each of us - whosoever believes in him, should not perish, but have everlasting life. A pathway to true and lasting transformation. Transformation that equips us for life on earth and prepares us for life in heaven.

Now there was a man of the Pharisees named Nicodemus, a ruler of the Jews. This man came to Jesus by night and said to him, "Rabbi, we know that you are a teacher come from God, for no one can do these signs that you do unless God is with him." Jesus answered him, "Truly, truly, I say to you, unless one is born again he cannot see the kingdom of God." Nicodemus said to him, "How can a man be born when he is old? Can he enter a second time into his mother's womb and be born?" Jesus answered, "Truly, truly, I say to you, unless one is born of water and the Spirit, he cannot enter the kingdom of God." John 3:1-36

Jesus himself invites us to take this journey of transformation with him: *"Come to me all you who are weary and carry heavy burdens, and I will give you rest. Take my yoke upon you, let me teach you, because I am humble and gentle at heart and you will find rest for your souls. For my yoke is easy to bear and the burden I give you is light"*- Matt.11:28-30 (NLT)

WHATEVER STATE I AM IN, I AM CONTENT

Philippians 4:11-12 - Not that I speak in respect of want: for I have learned, in whatsoever state I am, [therewith] to be content

1 Corinthians 7:17 - But as God hath distributed to every man, as the Lord hath called every one, so let him walk. And so ordain I in all churches.

Hebrews 13:5 - Let your conversation be without covetousness; and be content with such things as ye have: for he hath said, I will never leave thee, nor forsake thee.

Luke 12:15 - And he said unto them, Take heed, and beware of covetousness: for a man's life consisteth not in the abundance of the things which he possesseth.

Philippians 4:19 - But my God shall supply all your need according to his riches in glory by Christ Jesus.

Matthew 6:33 - But seek ye first the kingdom of God, and his righteousness; and all these things shall be added unto you.

Isaiah 26:3 - Thou wilt keep him in perfect peace, whose mind is stayed on thee: because he trusteth in thee.

2 Corinthians 12:10 - Therefore I take pleasure in infirmities, in reproaches, in necessities, in persecutions, in distresses for Christ's sake: for when I am weak, then am I strong.

Hebrews 13:6 So we say with confidence, "The Lord is my helper; I will not be afraid. What can mere mortals do to me?"

Psalms 37:3-5 - Trust in the LORD, and do good; so shalt thou dwell in the land, and verily thou shalt be fed.

"The LORD is my strength and my song, and he has become my salvation; this is my God, and I will praise him, my father's God, and I will exalt him."
Exodus 15:2

SOLUTIONS WEAR OUT, BUT GOD DOES NOT

BY THE RIVERS OF BABYLON

NO VISA REQUIRED

SOLUTIONS WEAR OUT, BUT GOD DOES NOT

Escaping from Egypt was the huge challenge facing the Children of Israel. The dream had become a nightmare. The place of refuge had become a place of pain and the people who had been so hospitable at the start, had become hostile in the extreme. The solution had become a problem.

Centuries before, faced with a severe famine that had visited untold hardship upon Jacob and his clan, relief was found in the prosperous state of Egypt. God had so engineered it that Jacob's son Joseph, who had been sold by his brothers into slavery, had ended up as the most powerful man in Egypt. He used his influence to give Jacob and his family 'permanent residence' in Egypt, they got their 'green cards.'

"And God spoke to Israel in the vision of the night..... and He said, I am God, the God of thy father, fear not to go down into Egypt; for I will there make thee a great nation. I will go down with thee into Egypt, and I will also bring thee up again . . . And Pharaoh spoke unto Joseph......The land of Egypt is before thee; in the best of the land make thy father and brethren to dwell....... And Israel dwelt in the land of Egypt, in the country of Goshen; and they had possessions therein, and grew, and multiplied exceedingly." (Genesis 47&48)

But as time progressed, the welcome wore out, their status changed from highly favored to barely tolerated, and they were kept for the labor they provided in slave-like conditions. They lived as second class citizens in a country to which they did not belong.

Egypt was a temporary solution, it was never intended to be their home. That which had been a great and miraculous solution had become a great and terrible problem. Canaan was their permanent solution, it was to be their home. To get there, they had to leave Egypt. They had to cross the wilderness. They had to fight powerful enemies. They had to fight and overcome their 'Egyptian' instincts and appetites. They had to be transformed.

The journey to Canaan is a story of transformation. It is an object lesson for us as Christians about the powerful enemies we will encounter on our journey; about the powerful forces within us that battle against the expressed will of God for our lives. It is also about an even more powerful God, whose promises never fail, who goes with us into our Egypt, travels with us through our wildernesses and will take us into our promised land.

Along the way, He provides solutions to the crises we face. Sometimes these solutions expire, they may even become problems themselves, but the God who is leading us, is already preparing an escape and engineering the next solution.

As the anxious and murmuring people, stood on the banks of Jordan, paralyzed by fear, God's servant Moses spoke these immortal words: "Fear ye not, stand still, and see the salvation of the Lord, which He shall show you today: for the Egyptians whom you see today, ye shall see them again no more for ever. The Lord shall fight for you and you shall hold your peace" - Genesis 14: 13&14 (KJV)
Don't be intimidated by Pharaoh, his chariots, his horses or his men, leave your battles to the Lord, He will fight for you.

BY THE RIVERS OF BABYLON

(Reflections on Psalm 137: 1-4 on the occasion of Jamaica's Fiftieth Anniversary)

Jamaica, the land of my birth, is a land of song. We celebrate our victories, we mourn our losses, we express our joys, we share our pain, we chastise our government, we educate our children, and we tell our story in song. Our songs may be boisterous and loud, or gentle and soft, but always colourful and always rooted in the reality of our experiences as a people and as a nation. Sometimes the song eludes us. Should we triumphantly celebrate, or should we lament . . .

Each of us, individually, yearn for song. A song that faces our situation realistically, acknowledging the good as well as the bad; but more than acknowledging, a song that inspires and encourages. A song that expresses our better selves, charts a better way. A song that corrects and consoles, exposes and empowers. A song that lifts up our heads and lightens our loads. A song that reaches us in our present reality and points and prompts us to a better place.

Psalm 137 identifies with this search for a song. In plaintive tones and emotionally loaded words, the Psalmist asks: "... how can we sing the Lord's song in a foreign land?" How can a people, exiled from their homeland, torn from family and the familiar, sitting sorrowfully by the rivers of Babylon, their instruments of music hung upon the willows . . . Silent. How can they sing? How can they find music in this strange and inhospitable place? How can they find music in the pain and despair of their new reality?

It is the cry of all exiled people, people confronting a new environment, one of dramatic differences and new challenges, a land where a song is called for from the oppressed, by their oppressors. The Melodians, a veteran Jamaican Reggae singing group, in their unique way and with their own particular interpretation, put this Psalm to music and to the timeless rhythm of the island, drawing powerful parallels between the experience of the people on the banks of the river Babylon and us, children of a displaced people.

But we can find our song in the strange land. A song not for the oppressors, but for ourselves and for our children. A song to make the long nights shorter, the dark days brighter, the difficult journey easier and the weary traveler stronger.

Our fore-parents, as they struggled in the cane fields of Jamaica under the watchful eyes of slave drivers with their ever-present whips, found their song. A song of freedom in spite of their chains. a song of hope in spite of their pain. A song of victory in spite of oppression.

It was not always easy to sing their song. It was not always even possible. But one day the chains fell off. The yoke was broken and a new day dawned. A day of freedom

Later as they ganged together to cultivate their small plots of land on some rocky hillside as free men and women they encouraged each other with work songs that gave rhythm to labor, fellowship to work and a common purpose in their journey to a new Jamaica. A Jamaica where all are free, and all are equal. Where each person is given a fair opportunity to use their God-given abilities to build a better life for themselves and a better future for their children,

In moments of loss and grief, as family and friends would gather in the home to 'set up', they would comfort each other with songs like; 'Rock of Ages cleft for me, in tunes and phrasings not always in keeping with the original, but always heartfelt and passionate.

We may not have the religious history that informed the Psalmist. We may not have a physical Jerusalem to remember, but we are a people of faith. Our belief in God has been part and parcel of our story as a people. In an age of political correctness and in an era when religion is dismissed as a part of the problem and not as a source of solutions, Jamaica stands as a nation and a people who recognize that there is a place for God in our national discourse and in the conduct of our affairs.

In 1962, as the "new nation" Jamaica, grasped its independence, took charge of its future and sought to chart a way forward, our leaders sought for a song, an Anthem, a rallying cry. In words immortal, they placed our fledging nation into the hands of our Eternal Father. Today that song challenges us to stand up for justice and truth, to act with respect for all, to cherish the weak and to respond to the call of duty, in the cause of *Jamaica, Land we love*.

As we sit on the banks of our respective *"Rivers of Babylon"* let us take our harps from off the willows, and let us get up and fight whilst we make music like our forefathers. Let us learn to sing the Lord's song, in whatever land we find ourselves, because He continues to guard us with His mighty hand.

NO VISA REQUIRED

In my country, Jamaica, as it is with countries across the world, Citizens don't need a Visa to enter. We don't need to show "return tickets". We don't have to show hotel reservations, or funds to "cover our stay". We can't be deported or denied entry, we belong here. We can be locked up, but we can't be deported.

It's a great feeling to belong somewhere. To know that we are a part of a community, that we are not alone in the world, that there are other people like us, sharing similar characteristics. As Christians however, our country is not our only home. We are proud to be citizens of "the greatest country in the world", but we are destined for a better place. A place for those who have turned away from sin, accepted His forgiveness and allowed him to place His mark of citizenship on them.

A place where one's Address does not matter. Colour does not matter. Education does not matter. Politics does not matter. Wealth does not matter. Age does not matter. Looks does not matter. Family history does not matter. "Connections" do not matter. "Papers" do not matter. Nothing matters except our relationship with God.

John described it in the Revelations: "*And I saw the Holy City, the New Jerusalem, coming down out of heaven from God, prepared and ready like a bride dressed to meet her husband. I heard a loud voice speaking from the throne: " now God's home is with human beings! He will live with them, and they shall be His people. God Himself will be with them, and he will be their God. He will wipe away all tears from their eyes. There will be no more death, no more grief or crying or pain. The old things have disappeared....And now I make all things new... Write this because it is true and can be trusted...*" Rev.21:2-5 (GNT)

I Pray that as each of us waits in the in-transit lounge of life, we make sure that our spiritual travel requirements are in order, so that when our name is called up yonder, we won't be told... *Entry Denied!*

GOD's WAY, ALL THE WAY

Psalms 46:10 - Be still, and know that I am God: I will be exalted among the heathen, I will be exalted in the earth.

Joshua 23:7 - 8 ... so that you will not associate with these nations, these which remain among you, or mention the name of their gods, or make anyone swear by them, or serve them, or bow down to them. But you are to cling to the LORD your God, as you have done to this day.

1 Samuel 12:21 You must not turn aside, for then you would go after futile things which cannot profit or deliver, because they are futile.

1 Corinthians 16:13 - Watch ye, stand fast in the faith, quit you like men, be strong.

Deuteronomy 31:6 Be strong and of a good courage, fear not, nor be afraid of them: for the LORD thy God, he it is that doth go with thee; he will not fail thee, nor forsake thee.

1 Corinthians 10:13 There hath no temptation taken you but such as is common to man: but God is faithful, who will not suffer you to be tempted above that ye are able; but will with the temptation also make a way to escape, that ye may be able to bear it.

Psalms 31:24 Be of good courage, and he shall strengthen your heart, all ye that hope in the LORD.

1 Corinthians 15:58 Therefore, my beloved brothers, be steadfast, immovable, always abounding in the work of the Lord, knowing that in the Lord your labor is not in vain.

John 16:33 I have said these things to you, that in me you may have peace. In the world you will have tribulation. But take heart; I have overcome the world.

Matthew 10:28 And do not fear those who kill the body but cannot kill the soul. Rather fear him who can destroy both soul and body in hell.

"I hereby command you: Be strong and courageous; do not be frightened or dismayed, for the Lord your God is with you wherever you go" - Joshua 1:9

BABYLON BY FAITH

FIREPROOF FAITH

THE LOVE THAT WILL NOT LET YOU GO

BABYLON BY FAITH

The Book of Daniel is one of the most familiar books of the Bible. The book takes us into the lives of the Children of Israel living as exiles in Babylon. It uses the experiences of Daniel and his friends to give us a window into that world.

It is a book that reverberates with the power of God at work in unusual ways, in an unlikely place. It starts with God's people on the losing end of wars. Losing their possessions, their pride, their independence and many of them being taken away as captives to serve their masters in Babylon.

God's people who had been the envy of their neighbours. God's people who had won battles without lifting a sword. God's people who had inspired fear among their enemies, because of the supernatural protection He gave them, had become defeated and powerless. They were overwhelmed by the power and might of Nebuchadnezzar, and his Babylonian army.

Their rebelliousness and sinfulness had exhausted God's patience and mercy. They had been warned many times of the consequences of their choices. Prophets had called for repentance and a return to the God of their fathers many times, but their calls were ignored and rejected.

They forgot that it was God that had taken them out of Egypt. Taken them through the wilderness. Taken them through the Red Sea and across the Jordan. It was God that had defeated their enemies and had given them a rich and fertile land. They had "arrived". God was ancient history. He was no longer relevant to them in their prosperity and self-sufficiency.

God had exhausted speech and had now resorted to action. His prophets had foretold that judgement would come, and it came. It came at the violent hands of Nebuchadnezzar. God's judgement was swift and severe. The price of their disobedience and rebelliousness was higher than they could have imagined, and more than they could bear.

It was in this climate of chaos and destruction that Daniel and his friends were carted off to Babylon, to face an unknown and possibly devastating future. They had lost the security of family, the protection of their leaders, and the resources of their religion. This was not a good start and the road ahead promised to get worse, rather than better.

Although they had left the temple behind however, the God of the temple was with them. They had grown up in an ungodly and evil society, so evil that it had earned God's wrath. Yet somehow they had developed deep and personal commitments to God and to His principles. Neither the ungodliness and sinfulness of their country, nor the evil and heathenish practices of their captors, the Babylonians, would rob them of this abiding faith in Yahweh their God.

Time after time, test after test, they chose God's way above the Babylonian way. They chose the hard and sometimes lonely path of faithfulness to God, over the easy and popular path of compromise and hypocrisy. They took their stand for God, and time after time, test after test, God took His stand for them.

"Then the king interviewed them and among them all none was found like Daniel, Hananiah, Mishael, and Azariah; therefore they served before the king. And in all matters of wisdom and understanding about which the king examined them, he found them ten times better than all the magicians and astrologers who were in all his realm. Thus Daniel continued to the first year of Cyrus" - Daniel 1:19-21 (NKJV)

FIREPROOF FAITH

Even though Daniel is the character whose story seems to be the centerpiece of the Book of Daniel, the stories of his friends are equally important and relevant to us today. Together with Daniel, they made the choice early in their 'Babylonian journey', not to defile themselves with certain elements of Babylonian life, that they felt would compromise their relationship with their God. They chose God's way over the Babylonian way.

However, choices have consequences and whereas they had control over their choices, and to some degree their actions, they had little or no control over the consequences. Their choices and their faith were not a mindless and sentimental impulse. They were fully aware of the possible consequences of their choices when they made them.

Their heroic decision not to bow to Nebuchadnezzar's great statue was virtually signing their own death sentence. The King had summoned all the leaders and officials in Babylon to the dedication of this massive golden statue. It was a major event with all the trappings and ceremonial elements that one would expect, in what was the richest and most powerful nation at the time.

Again, they had to choose. Do they blend in with the crowd, do they excuse themselves by saying we are only doing our official duty. Do they bow today and appeal to God for forgiveness tomorrow? It is not easy to go against the crowd. It is difficult to go against the orders of one's boss or king. It is however, dangerous and even tragic to go against a king who has absolute power and is regarded as a tyrant.

They considered their options and made their choice. They would not bow. The choice was a powerful expression of their faith in God, but their reasoning was a powerful demonstration of their commitment to Him.

Their faith in Him assured them that He could deliver them out of the fiery furnace, but their commitment to Him prepared them to accept any consequence that would have resulted. Their faith was not one dimensional. It was not faith on easy street in the land of plenty. It was faith in the face of fire. Faith that rested in absolute trust in the love and faithfulness of God. It was fireproof faith. Faith that the fire could not burn and faith that death could not destroy. Faith that embraced the consequences whether they were good or bad.

Their immortal words challenge and inspire us today: *"Shadrach, Meshach, and Abed-Nego answered and said to the king, O Nebuchadnezzar, we have no need to answer you in this matter. If that is the case, our God whom we serve is able to deliver us from the burning fiery furnace, and He will deliver us from your hand, O king. But if not, let it be known to you, O king, that we do not serve your gods, nor will we worship the golden image which you have set up"* – Daniel 3:16-18 (NKJV)

THE LOVE THAT WILL NOT LET YOU GO

There are times when our faith in God comes face to face with the roadblocks of seemingly unanswered prayers. Face to face with the roadblocks of a seemingly cold and uncaring God. Face to face with the roadblocks of shattered expectations, destroyed lives and hopeless futures. Face to face with the unexpected and unwelcome loss of someone we love and for whom we prayed. Face to face with a sense of emptiness and loss that seems eternal. Face to face with heartbreak and the agonizing anguish of a sorrowful soul.

In those moments, we join the millions who have trusted God, but find themselves questioning the wisdom of that trust, stuck with the seemingly unanswerable question, God why?

These are the valley experiences of life, the cloud that gives way to rain. The night that heralds the dawn of a new day. The death that makes way for new life. But in the valley, we cannot see the purpose. In the dark clouds, we cannot see the good. In the night, we cannot see the way forward.

Our pain numbs us, and our tears cloud our vision. But God is there all the time. The God who loved us enough to send his son to spill his own blood for us, is the God who feels our pain, hears our cries of anguish, witnesses our struggle to believe, and loves us even when we declare him unwelcome. He is with us in the dark nights of our soul.

Impossible as it may seem, and unreasonable as it may appear, there is a song in our pain, a poem in our distress and worship in our weeping. In times of joy and celebration, we easily burst out into singing:
". . . then sings my soul, my savior Lord to thee, how great thou art . . ." flows effortlessly from our lips. In the dark nights of the soul however, as pain plays havoc with our faith and joy is foreign to the ear, through the torment and tears, we can still sing, haltingly, faintly, even weakly: ". . . Then sings my soul my savior God to thee, how great thou art, how great thou art . . ." To the ears of our loving Father, it is music sweeter than any angelic chorus, than any earthly choir, it is the true music of the soul.

Many of us have had our valley experiences, our dark nights of the soul, when like the Psalmist we wish we had the wings of a dove so we could fly away. But no matter where we are or where we go, there is a love that pursues us. It is the unfailing love of God. A love that glows in the darkness of our nights and whispers in the tumults of our pain. A love discovered when our faith is tested. A love that will not let us go. This is the greatest love of all. It is my prayer that you will treasure this love as your most precious possession, and experience it for yourself if you have not yet done so.

O love that will not let me go, I rest my weary soul in thee;
I give back the life I owe, that in thine ocean depths it's flow may richer fuller be.

O Light that followest all my way, I yield my flickering torch to thee;
My heart restores it's borrowed ray, That in thy sunshine's blaze it's day, may brighter, fairer be.

O Joy that seekest me through pain, I cannot close my heart to thee;
I trace the rainbow through the rain, And feel the promise is not vain that morn shall tearless be.

O Cross that liftest up my head, I dare not ask to fly from thee;
I lay in dust life's glory dead, and from the ground there blossoms red, Life that shall endless be.

STAND FIRM IN THE FAITH

Hebrews 10:23 Let us hold fast the confession of our hope without wavering, for he who promised is faithful.

1 Corinthians 4:2 Now it is required that those who have been given a trust must prove faithful.

1 Corinthians 16:13 Be on guard. Stand firm in the faith. Be courageous. Be strong.

James 1:12 Blessed is the man who remains steadfast under trial, for when he has stood the test he will receive the crown of life, which God has promised to those who love him.

Hebrews 10:35-36 So do not throw away your confidence; it will be richly rewarded. You need to persevere so that when you have done the will of God, you will receive what he has promised.

Psalm 112:6-7 Surely the righteous will never be shaken; they will be remembered forever. They will have no fear of bad news; their hearts are steadfast, trusting in the LORD.

Romans 4:19-20 Without weakening in his faith, he faced the fact that his body was as good as dead—since he was about a hundred years old—and that Sarah's womb was also dead. Yet he did not waver through unbelief regarding the promise of God, but was strengthened in his faith and gave glory to God.

1 Samuel 12:21 You must not turn aside, for then you would go after futile things which can not profit or deliver, because they are futile.

Joshua 23:8 But you are to cling to the LORD your God, as you have done to this day.

Psalm 57:7 My heart, O God, is steadfast, my heart is steadfast;

At the same time the Spirit also helps us in our weakness, because we don't know how to pray for what we need. But the Spirit intercedes along with our groans that cannot be expressed in words."
- Romans 8:26

THE STEADFAST LOVE OF THE LORD NEVER CEASES

A FORGIVING GOD FOR A FORGETTING PEOPLE

DELIVERED FROM DISTRESS

THE STEADFAST LOVE OF THE LORD NEVER CEASES

In these times of extreme challenges and difficulties, it is natural to become anxious and concerned about our present situation and about the future. We try to find various ways of coping. We brace ourselves for the worst and we pray that divine intervention will turn the tide in our favor.

We pray and we plead with God for deliverance, but many times we feel as if it is a one-way conversation. Our faith is tested and we begin to wonder if God really hears, and if He does, does He really care? Some persons lose patience with God and walk away from Him. But He hears and He cares.

The God of our mountains is also the God of our valleys. He is equally present in our times of triumph and celebration, as He is in our times of defeat and discouragement.

Our pain is a part of His process to lead us into our purpose. It may not appear to be so, and it may sound like Christian "mumbo jumbo", but many people have testified to discovering God in the depth of their trials and adversities. They do not deny the painfulness of the path, they do not claim to have gone through with constant shouts of praise, and many will admit to having felt like giving up several times. But He calls us in difficult times to discover the power of enduring faith, the faith that will not let go, the faith that keeps holding on.

Lamentations 3, expresses the unimaginable suffering of one who felt abandoned by God. One who was trapped in a world of unending suffering and inescapable pain. It carries an underlying tone of desperation and hopelessness. But in the middle, like the sun breaking through dark and dismal storm clouds, are the transforming words: "The steadfast love of the Lord never ceases."

Wherever you are at this time, remember God is there with you and He will stay with you, and when you have come through, He will continue to be with you. I encourage you to meditate on the passage of Scripture highlighted, and to go beyond to reading the entire chapter and discover the power of our God's unfailing love.

"Remember my affliction and my wanderings, the wormwood and the gall! My soul continually remembers it and is bowed down within me. But this I call to mind, and therefore I have hope: The steadfast love of the Lord never ceases, his mercies never come to an end; they are new every morning; great is your faithfulness. The Lord is my portion, says my soul, therefore I will hope in him. The Lord is good to those who wait for him, to the soul who seeks him. It is good that one should wait quietly for the salvation of the Lord"
- Lamentations 3:19-26 (ESV)

A FORGIVING GOD FOR A FORGETTING PEOPLE

The Book of Deuteronomy is loaded with insight into Gods dealings with the Children of Israel. His love for them. His generous provisions and promises given to them and his requirement that they follow him exclusively.

We also see their reluctance to trust God. Their unbelief, murmuring and rebelliousness. The relationship between God and his people was a turbulent one. They were constantly griping about their living conditions and frequently used God's act of delivering them from Egypt as a reason to curse him.

They seem to have forgotten the pain and hardships of life in Egypt. They forgot that they were slaves in Egypt. Forced to work under harsh conditions with no Human Rights Agencies to monitor their condition, or Unions to bargain for better conditions. They forgot the cruelty of Pharaoh and his attempts to destroy all the male babies, including having them thrown to their deaths in the River Nile. They forgot how hard Pharaoh resisted Moses' effort to get them out of Egypt and Pharaoh's desperate attempt to recapture them.

They talked about the 'good life' in Egypt, the garlics and the onions that flavored their exquisite meals. One would get the impression that Egypt was for them a world class resort where they lived in comfort and ease. One cannot help but regard them as an extremely ungrateful people. But they were God's chosen people, stubborn, rebellious 'stiff-necked' as Moses called them, but God's people.

If we examine ourselves however, we may be surprised to discover how much like them we really are. We like our own way, we resist God's instruction, we doubt him, we question him, we are reluctant to do what he expects of us and we often fail to acknowledge, with gratitude, his many blessings on our lives.

But we are his people. Stubborn and rebellious, but his people. He gave his life for us because he loves us. He knows that behind our rebelliousness and doubt, our hearts long for him. Long for his presence, for his affirmation and for his redemptive love. Like the children of Israel, we can turn to him in our most trying times, in the storms of our own making, and find in Him, a loving God who never abandons His own.

"But from there you will seek the Lord your God, and you will find Him if you search for Him with all your heart and all your soul. When you are in distress and all these things have come upon you, in the latter days you will return to the Lord your God and listen to His voice. For the Lord your God is a compassionate God; He will not fail you nor destroy you nor forget the covenant with your fathers which He swore to them... Know therefore today, and take it to your heart, that the Lord, He is God in heaven above, and on the earth below: there is no other" - Deuteronomy 4:29-31, 39 (NASV)

DELIVERED FROM DISTRESS

In *Psalm 18* we witness David's song to God after he had been delivered from the hands of his arch-enemy Saul. It is a powerful Psalm in which David bares his soul to God. It is emotion-packed and filled with drama.

David did not hide his dilemma and distress with meaningless words. He was open and expressive in describing his desperate situation and the real trauma and emotional pain that he was experiencing at the hands of his enemies.

This was not David on his harp, singing and making melody to the Lord. This was not David walking in green pastures. This was not David basking in the sunshine of God's favour. This was David at the end of his rope, out of options, out of support and facing a horrible end. This was David in the valley of the shadow of death, where "the pangs of death surrounded me and the floods of ungodliness made me afraid."

But David found the key to his deliverance. A key that is available to God's children facing distress of the most extreme kind. David's key is found in verse 6 of the Psalm: " . . . in my distress I called upon the Lord, and cried out to my God; He heard my voice from His temple."

God responded powerfully. Demonstrating His might and authority over the earth and over David's enemies. He brought him deliverance. "He sent from above, He took me; He drew me out of many waters. He delivered me from my strong enemy, from those who hated me, for they were too strong for me... He also brought me out into a broad place; He delivered me because He delighted in me."

One cannot read this Psalm without being impressed with the nature of David's relationship with God, the confidence he had in Him, and in the strength of their relationship. It seemed to have been the source of his ability to endure the calamities and oppressive conditions that he faced.

It was not a distress-based relationship. It was a delight-based relationship. He delighted in God and God delighted in him. In his distress, God delivered him, because he delighted in God. Let us seek to have the kind of relationship with God that David had. One based on delight and not distress. One where our lives please God and invites His delight and favour.

"For you will light my lamp; the Lord will enlighten my darkness. For by you I can run against a troop, by my God I can leap over a wall. As for God His way is perfect, the word of the Lord is proven; He is a shield to all who trust in Him"- Psalms 18:28-30 (NKJV)

ABIDING IN THE SHADOW OF THE ALMIGHTY

Psalm 91: *"Whoever dwells in the shelter of the Most High will rest in the shadow of the Almighty.*

I will say of the LORD, He is my refuge and my fortress, my God, in whom I trust."

Surely he will save you from the fowler's snare and from the deadly pestilence.

He will cover you with his feathers, and under his wings you will find refuge; his faithfulness will be your shield and rampart.

You will not fear the terror of night, nor the arrow that flies by day, nor the pestilence that stalks in the darkness, nor the plague that destroys at midday.

A thousand may fall at your side, ten thousand at your right hand, but it will not come near you.

You will only observe with your eyes and see the punishment of the wicked.

If you say, "The LORD is my refuge," and you make the Most High your dwelling, no harm will overtake you, no disaster will come near your tent.

For he will command his angels concerning you to guard you in all your ways; they will lift you up in their hands, so that you will not strike your foot against a stone.

You will tread on the lion and the cobra; you will trample the great lion and the serpent.

"Because he loves me," says the LORD, "I will rescue him; I will protect him, for he acknowledges my name.

He will call on me, and I will answer him; I will be with him in trouble, I will deliver him and honor him.

With long life I will satisfy him and show him my salvation."

"The LORD your God is in your midst, a mighty one who will save; he will rejoice over you with gladness; he will quiet you by his love; he will exult over you with loud singing" - Zephaniah 3:17

A HIGHER CALLING

ALIVE IN CHRIST

SHAKEN BUT NOT STIRRED

A HIGHER CALLING

The *Apostle Paul* is one of the most outstanding characters in the New Testament, and in the Bible as a whole. His Letters, written thousands of years ago, still influence the lives of millions of persons around the world. His pioneering work as an Evangelist, led to the rapid expansion of the early Christian church and its establishment as a major world religion.

He was far from perfect however. Some people found him abrasive and tactless. Others found him a less-than inspiring speaker. His passionate commitment to the Jewish faith led him to persecuting Christians and he was among those who watched as Stephen was being stoned to death for his faith. His name drove fear into the hearts of Christians and he was regarded as one of the worst enemies of the church.

He felt that his calling was to defend the Jewish faith by any means necessary, and to destroy any and all opposition to it. He pursued this calling with great passion. He discovered along the way, that this was a wrong calling. He was fighting the wrong battle. He was engaged in a futile endeavor. An enterprise that was bound to fail and to leave him empty at the end of his days. He was kicking against the pricks.

Then one day his life was turned upside down. He was stopped in his tracks, and experienced a radical change in his life. It was the day that he met Christ. From that day, his life was changed. He no longer wanted to persecute Christians. He became a Christian instead. He no longer wanted to defend the Jewish faith by any means necessary. He had found a new life and with it a new calling. The right calling; a higher calling; a calling for which he could live, and a calling for which he was prepared to die.

Paul endured many hardships as a result of his calling. He encountered and endured hunger, beatings, sickness, shipwreck, imprisonment, and persecution of all types. But these did not dampen his passion, or his commitment to living his calling. For him, his calling to serve the Lord was his life. It was this passion for his calling that electrified people and inspired his writings and allowed God to use him so powerfully.

At the end of his life, he could say with calm assurance *"I have fought a good fight, I have finished the course, I have kept the faith."*

We may not experience the dramatic conversion of Paul, but once we have met Christ and accepted him as Lord, our lives will be changed. We will discover our calling, and by his grace, we can run our race, finish our course and with hand upraised in victory, declare that we have kept the faith.

ALIVE IN CHRIST

The act of being baptized in water is an indicator of a significant and life-changing decision, that each person made, before their public declaration of faith. They each became aware of their separation from God caused by sin, sought his forgiveness, repented of (turned away from) the old way of life that displeased God, and accepted the forgiveness that he extended to them. A forgiveness made possible by his sacrificial death on the cross.

This is not the act of man or woman, but the act of God. We do not have the power to forgive sin in ourselves, or in others. Our sin is an offense to God and He, the one offended, must be the one to extend the forgiveness. In this process of forgiveness, He removes the guilt of sin that each person carries, enters their life, and makes them new persons. That is what the Bible means when it says that, *"if any man be in Christ, he is a new creature, all things are passed away and behold all things become new."*

This new life is based on faith in Christ. It is not lived in our own strength or goodness. It is God's strength and God's goodness that enables us to live a life that pleases him. In this new life, Christ lives in us and lives through us.

Our ambitions become changed, as we give up our own agenda to embrace God's agenda for our lives. Our priorities change. We learn to, *"seek first the Kingdom of God."* Our relationships change. Christ becomes the center of our affection, and all other relationships are determined based on this reality. Our lives change, we discover like Paul that, "for me to live is Christ."

These changes do not happen overnight. But as we nurture this relationship with Christ, as we walk with him, converse with him, grow in our love for him, we become more like him. I welcome our brothers and sisters who have joined the family of believers and pray that together, we will become more and more like Christ, and experience the overflowing joy he provides for those that walk with him.

I encourage us all to reflect on the following testimony of the Apostle Paul, that reveals an important key to living victoriously as a Christian. *"I am crucified with Christ, nevertheless I live, yet not I, but Christ liveth in me and the life which I now live in the flesh I live by the faith of the Son of God, who loved me, and gave himself for me."* - Galatians 2:20 (KJV)

SHAKEN BUT NOT STIRRED

The prophet *Haggai*, in Haggai 2:6-9, spoke of a 'shaking' that was to come. It spoke of a time when the very foundations of society and the world would be shaken. This shaking would affect our lives as individuals in many areas, including our faith.

The evidence of this shaking is all around us. The world is in one of the most unstable and uncertain political periods in history. Countries that were friends or had agreed to peaceably co-exist, are suspicious of each other and are arming themselves in case war should break out. Economies that were strong, are displaying signs of weakness and many are unable to provide jobs and opportunities for their citizens, leading to unrest and instability. The European Union, one of the most important alliances in the world, is in danger of coming apart, and the world seems to be lurching from one crisis to another.

Societies and individuals are losing their moral compasses, causing many to throw their hands up in despair about the future of traditional institutions like the church, schools and families. Shared values and agreed standards of behavior are giving way to lifestyles governed by self-interest and personal preferences. The world is shaking, and the shaking impacts all of us.

But there is a basis for hope and reassurance in these unstable times. The reminder that God has provided a foundation for us in the person of Jesus Christ. He is to be our firm foundation, the rock on which we build our lives. He is the rock that will give us stability in times of uncertainty, security in times of threatening circumstances and resilience when the storms of life are raging.

No other foundation will do, and no other foundation is necessary. Our responsibility is to build well and to build wisely on this foundation. Even though we may feel the shocks of the shaking and have anxious moments as the world seems to wobble around us, we can live with confidence, knowing that Christ, our sure foundation, remains intact and secure.

"For we are God's fellow workers: you are God's field; you are God's building. According to the grace of God which is given to me. As a wise master builder I have laid the foundation, and another builds on it. But let each one take heed how he builds on it. For no other foundation can anyone lay than that which is laid, which is Jesus Christ" - 1 Corinthians 3:9-11 (NKJV)

OVERCOMING THROUGH COMMUNION WITH GOD

2 Corinthians 5:20 *Therefore, we are ambassadors for Christ, as though God were making an appeal through us; we beg you on behalf of Christ, be reconciled to God.*

1 Corinthians 1:9 *God is faithful, through whom you were called into fellowship with His Son, Jesus Christ our Lord.*

Romans 12:21 *But thanks be to God! He gives us the victory through our Lord Jesus Christ.*

1 Corinthians 15:57 *For everyone born of God overcomes the world. This is the victory that has overcome the world, even our faith.*

Hebrews 12:1 *No, in all these things we are more than conquerors through him who loved us.*

Romans 8:37 *You, dear children, are from God and have overcome them, because the one who is in you is greater than the one who is in the world.*

1 Peter 5:8 *But you, Lord, are a shield around me, my glory, the One who lifts my head high.*

Psalm 3:3 *Who is it that overcomes the world? Only the one who believes that Jesus is the Son of God.*

1 John 5:5 *The light shines in the darkness, and the darkness has not overcome it.*

John 1:5 *Fight the good fight of the faith. Take hold of the eternal life to which you were called when you made your good confession in the presence of many witnesses.*

1 John 5:4 *For no word from God will ever fail.*

"No testing has overtaken you that is not common to everyone. God is faithful, and he will not let you be tested beyond your strength, but with the testing he will also provide the way out so that you may be able to endure it." 1 Corinthians 10:13

HONESTLY GOD . . . THIS IS HOW I FEEL

FROM CONFLICT TO COMMUNION

LET THE BEAUTY OF JESUS BE SEEN!

HONESTLY GOD... THIS IS HOW I FEEL

Anger is one of the most common human emotions. The Oxford Dictionary describes it as extreme displeasure. All of us have experienced anger at some time or other.

Children get angry with their parents when they do not get to have their own way. Parents get angry with their children when they misbehave. Friends get angry with each other when they betray a trust. We get angry with ourselves when we fall short in some way.

But what about being angry with God?

If we are honest with ourselves, we will admit that there are times when we feel extreme displeasure towards God. Many people have lost faith in God, because they feel disappointed by Him in some way. However, our feelings of displeasure must be qualified by an understanding of who God is and our need to submit, difficult as it may be, to His will.

Job discovered this, and after passionately arguing with God about the severity of his suffering, he was forced to acknowledge that 'he spoke of things he did not understand' and that the ' plans of God would not be thwarted.' The severe trials he was experiencing were not punishment from an angry God, but a test. His faithfulness to God and his trust in Him was being tested.

The story of Lazarus is another glimpse into the experience of anger towards God. Martha was disappointed that Jesus delayed His visit to their ailing brother, and arrived days after he had died. When He arrived, Martha met him with the words, "if you were here, my brother would not have died". In other words, "Jesus, why did you take so long"? But even in her disappointment, she had an underlying faith and a hope, that somehow, Jesus would do something. She had lost her composure, but she had not lost her faith.

When we feel disappointed with God, when he takes too long to rescue us, when the prayer we have prayed seems to go unanswered, when our faith is rocked because we experience death rather than life, we can tell God how we feel. Like Martha we can say, if you were here, my life would be different. I would not be experiencing this pain. Why did you take so long? But through our tears and through our anger we must slowly accept that He is present, and where He is, life is possible. As one writer said:" He may be late, but He is right on time."

"After he had said this, he called out with a loud voice, Lazarus, come out! He came out, his hands and feet wrapped in grave cloths, and with a cloth around his face, untie him, Jesus told them, and let him go" - St. John 11:43-44 (TEV)

FROM CONFLICT TO COMMUNION

(Reflections on 1Corinthians 11:17-34)

Conflict is a feature of human interaction, from small arguments between children over toys, or some seemingly unimportant matter, to major wars causing the loss of millions of lives and the destruction of cities and nations. At the dawn of time, the "first family" was rocked by conflict, resulting in one brother murdering another.

Throughout history, attempts have been made to reduce conflict. To find ways of creating more harmonious relationships between people. To reduce the sources of conflict, and to prevent the escalation of conflict. But these have all fallen short, some have been abysmal failures.

The church is expected to be a place where love and peace prevail, and conflicts are rare. Even though both the Gospels and the Epistles devote a lot of attention to love and harmony, the sought after harmony seems elusive, and the people of God, continue to be plagued with conflicts.

Many conflicts have their roots in differences. Differences in age, size, wealth, status, ability, talents etc. can contribute to conflicts. But differences by themselves do not necessarily cause conflicts. Conflicts tend to arise when our differences are handled improperly.

In fact, selfishness is many times at the root of conflict. Our obsession with being right, with having it our way, with being first etc. can lead the most passive and docile of us into fits of rage and destructive conflicts. It thrives when we live according to the flesh, rather than live by the spirit.

Conflicts cause our differences to become divisions. We form cliques and parties. It was the problem at Corinth and is the problem in the Church today.

This gifted and important church of Corinth, had been a blessing and an Agent of Evangelism. But it was sabotaging itself because of the many conflicts and deep divisions that were there.

No Christian, no Church, no matter how gifted, can fulfill their potential and purpose, if they are being strangled by divisiveness. Paul's pain and anger was clear from the tone of his writing. He was deeply disturbed by the divisions and divisiveness in the church. He was even more disturbed by the fact this divisiveness and conflict was being wantonly played out in what should have been the showpiece of Christian harmony, unity and fellowship . . . the Lord's Supper.

The conflict was causing disgrace and damage to the name of Christ and pain and suffering to the Body of Christ. It was profaning this sacred event and tarnishing the memory of Christ. It was causing personal suffering and spiritual pain; the Church was being despised and the brethren humiliated.

The divisive and disgraceful behavior of the Corinthians when observing the Lord's Supper was robbing them, as a church and as individuals, of one of the richest and most blessed experiences available to human beings, the experience of Holy Communion. The privilege of sitting worthily at the Lord's Table, to dine with the King.

But Communion is not only possible, Communion is necessary.

The road to Communion starts with self-examination. We are advised that each man should examine himself. The Holy Spirit that lives within us is the "Chief Inspector", turning his searchlight on our lives, putting us under his microscope and showing us our true selves.

It requires putting self aside and being prepared to wait for each other. Not the mad scramble and crude grabbing of space and privilege that seemed to be common among the Corinthians. Waiting requires: seeing others not ignoring them, demonstrating care and concern, exercising restraint, delaying in the interest of others. Waiting shows confidence, God is not running away. Waiting allows us to realign our perspective, and re-discover that it is not about us, it is all about Him. In observing the Lord's Supper, we are proclaiming the Lord's death until He comes

A picture of Communion rediscovered is the disciples on the Emmaus road. They started the journey, discouraged, defeated and hopeless, but Jesus met them, walked with them, communed with them and transformed them. Their spirits that had been broken and paralyzed by pain were healed, their hearts burned within them. They made a "U-turn", back to Jerusalem, no longer discouraged and dejected, but excited and alive. It changed their plans, changed their direction, changed their lives. Communion transforms!

LET THE BEAUTY OF JESUS BE SEEN!

In a world scarred by sin and made ugly by the evil actions of men and women pursuing their own pleasures and ambitions, without regard for others, or for the God who made them, there is a desperate need for the beauty of Jesus.

A beauty that can reach the 'worst of sinners'. A beauty that can make the most violent opponent of the Gospel such as the writer of the cited passage was, become its most passionate promoter. A beauty that caused a scholar/academic with extremist tendencies, to proudly claim himself to be a fool for Christ.

The power of this passage is not only in its compelling words and irresistible logic, but in the instrument God used to deliver the words. The Apostle Paul was transformed from an unattractive zealot, whose very name drove fear into the hearts of believers, into a persuasive and inspirational messenger of the Gospel. One who brought the beauty of Jesus to a world enslaved by heathen philosophies, empty religions and corrupt lifestyles. A world very much like the one in which we live today.

Paul wrote to a people who had been touched by the beauty

of Jesus, and whose actions had brought joy and encouragement to an enslaved Paul. Reminding him of the beauty of Christian fellowship, at a time when many were corrupting the beautiful message by their selfish ambitions and insincerity.

He challenged them as he challenges us, thousands of years later, that they should allow the beauty of Jesus, the perfect Son of God and the incarnation of love, to be seen in them. Let it be seen in our lives, our families, our groups, our churches, our communities, our countries, our regions, our world.

The passage starts with an appeal to two faithful workers who were separated by conflict. A conflict that caused Paul great pain, and he pleaded with them to find agreement 'in the Lord.' But it was not just being left up to them, he was calling on mutual friends his 'true companions" to intervene and help to rebuild the broken relationship and restore harmony.

Conflicts and disagreements among the followers of Christ have been the greatest 'beauty robbers' of the gospel message. It is the virus that corrupts and disables the operating system of our groups, fellowship and ministries and churches. They hide the beauty of Jesus from those desperately searching for His beauty.

He told them then as he tells us today: "Agree with each other in the Lord" . . . so that the beauty of Christian harmony may be seen in us.

Imprisoned and in chains, robbed of his freedom, separated from the warmth of fellowship and the close support of other believers, Paul could be excused if he used the occasion to gripe and complain, but there is no evidence that he did. He had an irrepressible joy that neither prison, chains, nor an uncertain future could suppress. His call to rejoice is therefore not the empty words of a religious lightweight, but of someone who had been tested and had declared that all things work together for good. His words reverberated from the walls of his prison cell: Rejoice evermore, and again I say rejoice!

He told them then as he tells us today: "Rejoice always and again I say Rejoice"! . . . so that the beauty of Christian joy may be seen in us.

Anxiety is a condition that has been a part of the human experience from the beginning of time, and Christians, even the saintliest, are not spared from its attack. But Paul, who had experienced more than his fair share of life-threatening situations, and anxious moments, had discovered a powerful antidote to anxiety . . . PRAYER! It is his prescription for 'every situation.'

Prayer leads to the peace that is beyond understanding. The peace that protects the heart and guards the mind. In a world of anxious people drowning their anxieties with alcohol, medication, pleasure, and Godless spirituality, there has never been a greater need for this peace. He told them then, as he tells us today: "In every situation by prayer and petition, with thanksgiving, present your requests to God" . . . so, that the beauty of Christian Prayer may be seen in us.

One of the most powerful evidences in support of the Christian Gospel is transformed lives. All of us as Christians, are people with a past. Paul listed the former lives of the early Christians in 1 Corinthians 6:9-11, it reads like a rogue's gallery. They had been transformed into new creatures. They lived holy lives that stood in stark contrast to the sinful norms of the time. He presented his life as a model, and instructed them to put into practice, the lessons he had taught and demonstrated.

Today the beauty of the Gospel has been seriously blemished by high profile scandals involving Christian Leaders. It is further aggravated by the inconsistencies and hypocrisy of so many believers, whose lifestyles are a daily denial of the transforming power of Jesus Christ.

In a world of violence, war, conflict, strife, pain and anxiety, the promise of the prevailing presence of Christ and access through prayer to His life changing influence is not a promise to be ignored. This is a world that desperately needs to see the beauty of Jesus.

Our challenge, our prayer and our power, can be found in the words of this simple chorus:

Let the beauty of Jesus be seen in me
All his wondrous compassion and purity
Oh thou spirit divine all my nature refine
Till the beauty of Jesus be seen in me.

HOPE FOR TODAY, STRENGTH FOR TOMORROW

Psalm 71:5 For you have been my hope, O Sovereign LORD, my confidence since my youth

Psalm 33:22 May your unfailing love rest upon us, O LORD, even as we put our hope in you Psalm 9:18 But the needy will not always be forgotten, nor the hope of the afflicted ever perish

Psalm 146:5 Blessed is he whose help is the God of Jacob, whose hope is in the LORD his God

Psalm 78:7 Then they would put their trust in God and would not forget his deeds but would keep his commands

Jeremiah 17:7 But blessed is the man who trusts in the LORD, whose confidence is in him

Joel 3:16 The LORD will roar from Zion and thunder from Jerusalem; the earth and the sky will tremble. But the LORD will be a refuge for his people, a stronghold for the people of Israel

Psalm 39:7 But now, Lord, what do I look for? My hope is in you

Zechariah 9:12 Return to your fortress, O prisoners of hope; even now I announce that I will restore twice as much to you

Lamentations 3:26 It is good to wait quietly for the salvation of the LORD

"Then you will call on me and come and pray to me, and I will listen to you. You will seek me and find me when you seek me with all your heart" - Jeremiah 29:12-13

THE COMPASSION OF CHRIST

WILL YOU BE MADE WHOLE?

WHERE HE IS, THERE IS HOPE

THE COMPASSION OF CHRIST

As Jesus moved around, he was followed by huge crowds. He healed and taught with an aura and authority that was new to people. He must have been treated like a celebrity, a hero. He was much sought after, and in demand. Yet for the most part, he seemed unhurried, even casual at times, totally indifferent to the acclaim and attention he was getting.

His capacity to care was extraordinary. His actions were prompted by a love for people and a deep compassion for them. The writer of the Gospels often describe him as being, 'moved with compassion.' His compassion was not a mere emotional tug on his heart strings, a reaction to tear-jerking situations or the feigned sympathy of a Pharisee.

It was a deeply felt emotion that was not content to indulge itself with empty words and meaningless actions. It consumed his being and moved him. Moved him to take action to alter circumstances and change situations. His compassion addressed needs and changed lives.

His compassion led Him to heal the sick, restore sight to the blind, open the ears of the deaf, restore life to the dead, deliver persons held captive by demonic spirits, feed the hungry, comfort the sad, save the lost and bring wholeness to the broken. The story of Jesus is a story of compassion, a compassion that had no equal.

Each of us who have met Jesus and have been changed by him, are the beneficiaries of this compassion. We have discovered that his compassion broke through the walls of our sinfulness, our fears and doubts, our resistance to righteousness and our hardness of heart. We found his love and compassion irresistible.

Having benefitted so greatly from his compassion, we should express our gratitude to him by being compassionate to others. A compassion that others will find irresistible and so be attracted to this compassionate Christ who changes lives.

"John's disciples came and took his body and buried it. Then they went and told Jesus. When Jesus heard what had happened, he withdrew by boat to a solitary place. Hearing of this, the crowds followed him on foot from the towns. When Jesus landed and saw a large crowd, he had compassion on them and healed their sick" - Matthew 14:12-14 (NIV)

WILL YOU BE MADE WHOLE?

"When Jesus saw him lying there and knew that he had been now a long time in that condition, he said unto him, will you be made whole?" - St. John 5:5 (KJV 2000)

This question seems to be one of the most redundant questions in the Bible, possibly one of the most redundant questions ever asked. But it is not as redundant as it initially appears to be.

Most of us are familiar with the story. The man to whom Jesus was speaking had been lame for a long time, thirty-eight years in fact. He had been patiently waiting by the pool for his healing. To be healed, he needed to be the first to enter the water when the healing angel troubled it. So far, he had not been able to get into the water fast enough, and must have watched painfully as others got their healing and left celebrating their recovery and new lease on life.

He was surrounded by other persons also waiting to be healed. They were described as "a great multitude of impotent folk, of blind, halt and withered." They were his neighbors. The people he associated with on a daily basis. It is quite possible that after all these years they had adjusted to the situation, made themselves comfortable and "at home", as a community of 'sufferers' united in their lack and resigned to an uncertain future. For many, hope of healing, of leaving that place, of returning to the "world outside", had long since died. This was the life they knew. This was the world they mastered. This was the place where they were accepted as equals. This was the place they felt a sense of "belonging".

The existence of a lack, the presence of a need, does not necessarily mean that there is an equal desire to have the need met, or to be made whole. Jesus was right in asking the question "... will you be made whole?" In asking the question, He sends us an important message. He is telling us that we must first desire to be made whole before he can do His work of making us whole. We must first want to be changed, before we can become changed.

As a church, we must focus on 'transformation'. We want to experience change in our personal lives, in the lives of our families, our church and our community. But it starts with the desire. Our desire for change must be greater than the comfort and convenience of our present state. There must be a deep and passionate yearning for more. The Psalmist describes it as a "hungering and a thirsting".

In the story, the man did not answer the question "... will you be made whole?" But as many of us would have done, he explained away his situation. Mercifully, Jesus ignored his words and took the action he needed, Jesus healed him and made him whole. As you wait for the moving of the waters in your life, can you hear the voice of a gracious Saviour asking you, asking me "... will you be made whole?" I pray that each of us will hear Him and answer ... yes Lord, I want to be made whole, I want to be transformed into the person you designed me to be.

The story ends with the man who had no one to help him into the water, getting up in his own strength, taking up his bed and moving from the place of helplessness. There is always hope, not in some seasonal act of angels at some pool, but in the constant presence of our Lord, who promises never to leave us nor forsake us.

Great Is Thy faithfulness, O God my Father! There is no shadow of turning with Thee;
Thou changest not, Thy compassions, they fail not; As Thou hast been,Thou forever wilt be.
Great Is Thy faithfulness . . . Morning by morning new mercies I see;
All I have needed Thy hand hath provided; Great is Thy Faithfulness, Lord unto me!
[Great Is Thy Faithfulness, Thomas Chisholm – 1925]

WHERE HE IS, THERE IS HOPE

In these challenging times, it is very easy to become discouraged. Our environment seems to be filled with overwhelming challenges, many of them outside of our influence and control. We apply our skills, we use our resources and we exert great effort, but the results are slow in coming and may appear in some cases to be negative.

It is easy to lose hope. Easy to feel like "throwing in the towel. Easy to think that the fight is not worth it. But there is always HOPE. As one person said, "where there is life, there is hope." However, I believe a more useful statement is, "where there is God, there is hope."

This is demonstrated over and over again in the Bible and especially in the life of the Children of Israel. Isaiah was one of their most outstanding prophets, his name means, ' the eternal God is salvation.' His book speaks a lot about God's judgement, but it also contains some of the most inspiring words about God's redemptive love and salvation.

It is my prayer that the following select verses from Isaiah 51 will reassure you of God's presence, and remind you that where He is, there is hope.

"Listen to me, you who pursue righteousness, who seek the Lord: Look to the rock from which you were hewn, and the quarry from which you were dug. "Look to Abraham your father and to Sarah who gave birth to you in pain: when he was but one I called him, then I blessed him, and multiplied him." Indeed the Lord will comfort Zion; He will comfort all her waste places. And her wilderness He will make like Eden, and her desert like the garden of the Lord: Joy and gladness will be found in her, thanksgiving and the sound of a melody.

Pay attention to me, O My people, and give ear to Me, O My nation; For a law will go forth from Me, and I will set My justice for a light of the peoples; My righteousness is near and My salvation has gone forth and My arms will judge the people's; the coastlands will wait for Me, and for my arms, they will wait expectantly.

"Lift up your eyes to the sky, then look to the earth beneath; for the sky will vanish like smoke, and the earth will wear out like a garment and its inhabitants will die in like manner; but My salvation will be forever, and My righteousness will not wane.

So the ransomed (redeemed) of the Lord will return and come with joyful shouting to Zion and everlasting joy will be on their heads. They will obtain gladness and joy, and sorrow and sighing will flee away.

(Excerpts from Isaiah 51, New American Standard Version)

. . . FALLEN, BUT WE WILL RISE AGAIN

Psalm 37:23-24 The steps of a good man are ordered by the Lord: and he delighteth in his way. Though he fall, he shall not be utterly cast down: for the Lord upholdeth him with his hand.

Micah 7:8 Our enemies have no reason to gloat over us. We have fallen, but we will rise again. We are in darkness now, but the Lord will give us light.

Romans 3:23 For all have sinned and fall short of the glory of God

Psalm 51:10 Create in me a clean heart, O God, And renew a steadfast spirit within me.

Philippians 3:13-14 Brothers and sisters, I do not consider myself to have attained this. Instead I am single-minded: Forgetting the things that are behind and reaching out for the things that are ahead, with this goal in mind, I strive toward the prize of the upward call of God in Christ Jesus

Philippians 4:13 I can do all things through Christ who strengthens me.

Isaiah 40:30-31 Though youths grow weary and tired, And vigorous young men stumble badly, Yet those who wait for the LORD Will gain new strength; They will mount up with wings like eagles, They will run and not get tired, They will walk and not become weary.

Isaiah 40:29 He gives strength to the weary and increases the power of the weak.

2 Corinthians 5:17 Therefore if any man be in Christ, he is a new creature: old things are passed away; behold, all things are become new.

Ezekiel 36:26-27 Moreover, I will give you a new heart and put a new spirit within you; and I will remove the heart of stone from your flesh and give you a heart of flesh. "I will put My Spirit within you and cause you to walk in my statutes, and you will be careful to observe My ordinances.

"If you will only obey the Lord your God, by diligently observing all his commandments that I am commanding you today, the Lord your God will set you high above all the nations of the earth; all these blessings shall come upon you and overtake you, if you obey the Lord your God" - Deuteronomy 28:1-2

LORD, IT WAS ME

FAILING FORWARD

INNER STRENGTH

LORD, IT WAS ME

Accepting responsibility for our actions and the outcome of our actions is not always easy. Some would say rarely easy. Others would say, never easy. Recently I was reading in Genesis, and paused to reflect on the conversation God had with Adam and Eve after they had eaten the forbidden fruit.

Persuaded by the snake to 'emancipate' herself from a selfish God who had set up silly rules to keep man from becoming as enlightened as He was, she broke God's law and ate the fruit. Eve then made Adam an offer that he found irresistible and he joined her and he also ate the fruit.

The simple act dramatically changed the course of their lives and the history of mankind. They discovered their nakedness and with it, a sense of embarrassment, that resulted in them hiding from God. It was the start of a downward spiral. Deception led to disobedience, which led to denial and the result was a disaster that has brought pain and suffering to every generation of mankind since.

When God challenged Adam on his actions, he denied responsibility and passed the blame unto the 'woman that you gave me.' Eve in turn denied responsibility and passed the blame unto the snake. The snake was not around to speak for himself, but God had heard enough, and had had enough. He expelled them from the garden and placed them 'under discipline.'

I wonder how God would have responded to Adam and Eve, if they had with honesty and in a repentant manner, accepted responsibility for their actions. We will never know the answer, but the narrative of Scripture strongly suggests that God expects us to take responsibility for our actions. That denial and deceit are highly offensive to Him.

The story of Nehemiah is one of the most inspiring in the Old Testament, his life and actions have been studied by many and used as an example of outstanding leadership. He stands out as someone who did not try to shift blame or avoid responsibility. His prayer gives us an insight into his approach to situations, and his ability to acknowledge not only his own failings, but to share in ownership of the failings of others.

In each of our lives, there are persons who have helped us, hindered us and even hurt us. But we must reach a point in our lives where we acknowledge their roles and move on. They may influence, but they do not determine our lives. We must take responsibility for our actions and avoid the temptation to blame others and find excuses that appear to 'get us off the hook.' Let us not follow the tragic example of Adam, but the redemptive example of Nehemiah, that brought God's blessing not only on his own life, but on the lives of his people. Let us take full responsibility for who we are and where we are, and through the enabling of God, work to become the masterpiece He designed us to be.

"Let thine ear now be attentive, and thine eyes open, that thou mayest hear the prayer of thy servant, which I pray before thee now, day and night, for the children of Israel thy servants, and

confess the sins of the children of Israel, which we have sinned against thee: both I and my father's house have sinned. We have dealt very corruptly against thee, we have not kept thy commandments, nor the statutes, nor the judgements, which thou commandedst thy servant Moses."- Nehemiah 1 : 6-7 (KJV)

FAILING FORWARD

(Reference to the book, "Failing Forward" by Dr. John Maxwell)

All of us have failed at something at some point in our lives, it may have been an Exam, a job, an assignment, a relationship, a business, something small and unimportant, or something large and significant. The decisive factor is what we do when we fail.

Although failure is such a common experience, it is not a subject that is talked about a lot, or for which many books have been written. There seems to be a conspiracy of silence when it comes to failing. But whilst it is not something to be celebrated, it certainly is something that we should learn to understand and to deal with.

The ability to rebound from failure is an essential skill, if we are to succeed in any aspect of life. According to Dr John Maxwell in his book, Failing Forward: "the difference between average people and achieving people, is their perception of and response to failure."

In any Championship Final, two winners will enter the field of play, but only one will take the Cup. One will leave the field to the cheers of the crowd, celebrating their victory and the other will leave the field disappointed that they did not win, they failed. They may have failed to win the Match, but this will not be the end of their "Game". It is just the beginning of the next Game.

As we live our lives, let us have a healthy regard for our failures. They do not define us. They affect us and will influence us, but they do not determine our future. We should take our successes and failures in stride. Living in obedience and reliance on God.

"Jeremiah, say this to the people of Judah: 'This is what the Lord says: "'You know if a man falls down, he gets up again. And if a man goes the wrong way, he turns around and comes back" Jeremiah 8:4

"The righteous may fall seven times but still get up, but the wicked will stumble into trouble" Proverbs 24:16

Let us remember that, *"I can do all things who Christ which strengtheneth me."* Philippians 4:13 (KJV)

INNER STRENGTH

Strength is a quality that we all desire to have, and one that we admire in others. It is one of the qualities that we most often associate with leaders, heroes and persons we regard as successful. It has traditionally been associated with being physically strong and powerful. Characters like Samson, Goliath, Hercules, Atlas and others, are often cited as examples of physically strong persons.

But it is now widely acknowledged that strength is not restricted to the physical. We speak about emotional strength, spiritual strength, financial strength, mental strength and inner strength among others. According to the *Merriam Webster Dictionary, strength is: the quality of being physically strong / the ability to resist being moved or broken by a force / the quality that allows someone to deal with problems in a determined and effective way.*

Many of us cannot boast of being physically strong, or even aspire to be physically strong, but each of us can have our unique strengths. Each of us has the capacity for great inner strength, the strength that is not manifested in bulging biceps, the ability to lift heavy weights, or win physical fights. The strength that is not determined by gender, height, weight or age.

It is the strength that gives one the ability to resist being moved or being broken by a force. It was the strength demonstrated by the American Civil Rights Icon, Rosa Parkes, when she stood up to the might of institutional racism by refusing to give up her seat because she was black.

It was the strength that caused Jamaican National Hero and Baptist Preacher, Sam Sharpe, to fight against 'church sanctioned' slavery, and to declare; "I would rather die upon yonder gallows than live in slavery." It is the strength at work in millions of Christians across the world, who live in oppressive states where they suffer and in some cases are killed, because of their faith in Jesus Christ.

But strength is not only found in the lives of those we regard as exceptional, or those we regard as heroes. It is found in the lives of many ordinary Christians who refuse to be moved, or become broken by the forces of evil that are constantly working against them. Christians who are committed to following Christ.

This inner strength is the strength to fight despite weakness, to rejoice despite pain, to serve despite opposition, to reach out despite rejection, to give despite lack, to worship despite suffering and to love despite hate. It is a strength within us that comes from beyond us. It is a strength that comes from God. Let us draw support from the words of the Apostle Paul who found the source of his strength in Christ.

"And He said to me, My grace is sufficient for you, for my strength is made perfect in weakness. Therefore most gladly I will rather boast in my infirmities, that the power of Christ may rest upon me.
- 2 Corinthians 12:9 (NKJV)

BEARING WITNESS ALONG THE WAY...

2 Corinthians 13:5 *Examine yourselves, to see whether you are in the faith. Test yourselves. Or do you not realize this about yourselves, that Jesus Christ is in you?—unless indeed you fail to meet the test!*

Ephesians 5:1-2 *Be ye therefore followers of God, as dear children; And walk in love, as Christ also hath loved us, and hath given himself for us an offering and a sacrifice to God for a sweet smelling savour*

Romans 12:2 *And do not be conformed to this world, but be transformed by the renewing of your mind, so that you may prove what the will of God is, that which is good and acceptable and perfect*

Matthew 5:13-16 *"You are the salt of the earth, but if salt has lost its taste, how shall its saltiness be restored? It is no longer good for anything except to be thrown out and trampled under people's feet. "You are the light of the world. A city set on a hill cannot be hidden. Nor do people light a lamp and put it under a basket, but on a stand, and it gives light to all in the house. In the same way, let your light shine before others, so that they may see your good works and give glory to your Father who is in heaven.*

John 13:34-35 *A new command I give you: Love one another. As I have loved you, so you must love one another. By this everyone will know that you are my disciples, if you love one another*

1 Peter 3:15 *But in your hearts honor Christ the Lord as holy, always being prepared to make a defense to anyone who asks you for a reason for the hope that is in you; yet do it with gentleness and respect*

Proverbs 2:2 *Making your ear attentive to wisdom and inclining your heart to understanding;*

"Because he has focused his love on me, I will deliver him. I will protect him because he knows my name. When he calls out to me, I will answer him. I will be with him in his distress. I will deliver him, and I will honor him" - Psalm 91:14-15

DO YOU PUT PIGS FIRST?

CALLED TO BE SALT AND LIGHT

LEARNING TO LISTEN

DO YOU PUT PIGS FIRST?

There is a very compelling story in the Gospel of Mark (chapter 5), that demonstrates the conflict between good and evil. The conflict between Jesus Christ and the agents of the devil. It is the story of the healing of a demon-possessed man from the region of the Gerasenes and the unexpected response of the people to his healing and to Jesus the healer.

The man was known throughout the region for the severity of his condition. He was an outcast from society. His condition had alienated him from his family, his friends and his community. He now lived among the tombs and " no one could bind him anymore, not even with a chain. For he had often been chained hand and foot, but he tore the chains apart and broke the irons on his feet. No one was strong enough to subdue him, night and day among the tombs and in the hills, he would cry out and cut himself with stones."

He was a tormented and terrifying soul. But he was somebody's child. It is quite possible that he had a normal childhood, with loving parents, aunts and uncles and friends. They may have watched painfully as his life spun out of control, as he moved further and further away from them into a dark, and demon controlled world.

Then one momentous day he met Jesus Christ, who delivered him from the legion of demons that occupied and controlled his life. He experienced a miracle and his life was transformed virtually in an instant. According to Mark: "....they saw the man who had been possessed by the legion of demons, sitting, dressed and in his right mind."

The demons that had been slowly destroying his life had been cast out and had entered into two thousand (2000) pigs that were nearby. The pigs ran into the sea and drowned. This simple act of mercy on the part of Jesus had disrupted the economy. Threatened the livelihoods of the people and they 'were afraid."

Having witnessed this miracle, and the remarkable transformation of the man, one would have expected them to be overflowing with gratitude to Jesus and inviting him to stay a little longer. But this was not to be the case. They wanted Jesus out of their lives as fast as possible. It is clear that they were driven by the need to protect their material wealth. The miraculous transforming of lives was not on their list of priorities. They put pigs first!

We may look with disdain at their warped priorities, but many people are just like that today. Facilitating the transforming work of Christ is not a priority. They find him disruptive and dangerous. They fear that if they let him into their lives, if they encourage him to stay, they could lose the things they regard as valuable. They could lose their 'pigs,' and so they keep putting 'pigs' first.

Let us be cautioned by this story and embrace Jesus and his transforming power, and let us do all we can to facilitate his work of transformation in the lives of those around us. Let us not be like those people described by Mark the Apostle, who preferred that their fellow Citizen remain in a terrible and self- destructive situation, rather than experience the wholeness and restoration that Christ brings. Let us not put pigs first.

"Those who had seen it told the people what had happened to the demon possessed man, and told them about the pigs as well. Then the people began to plead with Jesus to leave their region." - Mark 5:17 (NIV)

CALLED TO BE SALT AND LIGHT

The world woke up to the reality that Voters in the United Kingdom had voted to leave the European Union (EU). For many, the unthinkable had happened. There had been serious warnings that a vote to leave, would have devastating consequences on the British economy, increase global political instability and could adversely affect the world economy.

Why does all this matter . . . and does it really? It does, because the frustration and fear that fueled the vote to leave the EU is rising all across the world. The prosperity and affluence that exists in some places and among some people, painfully contrasts with the poverty, suffering and hopelessness that is the lot of so many others, whether they live in rich "first world" countries or in poor underdeveloped countries.

The response of some people to a world seemingly spinning out of control, is to find some way of escaping the reality. Many drown their pain in alcohol, others numb themselves with narcotics, some hide their pain by "living large" and laughing loud. Many engage in reckless behavior. Others take on a "doomsday" approach and retreat to 'safe' places with bunkers stocked with supplies for the coming catastrophe. Some "escape" by embracing empty religions and spiritual practices that ignore reality and give them a false sense of peace.

As Christians, we are affected by these momentous happenings and may understandably experience our own share of frustration, anxiety and fear. But our response cannot be that of hiding or seeking to escape. We are called to be "salt and light". We are called to live out our faith in the real world. To use our God given abilities to function in a changing environment that is sometimes hostile to our faith. We would have learned not to put our confidence in man, or the institutions that he creates. Our trust must remain in the God who is the Eternal Lord. We can take guidance and encouragement from Paul's words to the 'experts' and sceptics in Athens:

"The God who made the world and everything in it is the Lord of heaven and earth and does not live in temples built with hands. And He is not served by human hands, as if he needed anything, because He Himself gives all men life and breath and everything else. From one man He made every nation of men, that they should inhabit the whole earth: and He determined the times set for them and the exact places that they should live. God did this so that men would seek him and perhaps reach out for Him and find Him, though He is not far from each of us. For in Him we live and move and have our being." - Acts 17: 24-28 (NIV)

LEARNING TO LISTEN

"Let the wise listen and add to their learning, and let the discerning get guidance." - Proverbs 1:4 (NIV)

We live in a noisy world. We are animated in our conversations. When we get going, talking becomes a 'full body' experience ...heads, shoulders, hands, feet all caught up in the rhythm of conversation. To the onlooker, many conversations would appear to be the opening round of a boxing match, until a burst of laughter, or some expression of comradeship punctuates the exchange.

We can talk persuasively and convincingly on topics that we may have only passing acquaintance with. Where we lack information, we compensate with conviction. We can advise Governments, Increase prosperity, reduce crime and heal ourselves and the world of all ills in the process.

We love to talk, and there is a beauty and an attractiveness to our conversations (for the most part). There is also a wisdom and practicality to our conversations. It is amazing to hear some individual who had not left the shores of their country, or been to an institution of higher learning speak knowledgeably on matters of international politics, science, philosophy and psychology.

Sometimes we talk, but we do not communicate. Meaning is lost in the abundance of words. Feelings are hidden in the richness of expressions. Relationships stagnate because words become barriers rather than bridges. Sometimes what we need is not more talking, but more listening.

Listening is an art that should be cultivated and nurtured. It does not come easily, especially on matters important to us, or areas in which we have much information or strong opinions. It requires discipline and the capacity to place the interest of others before our own. It is an art that I am struggling to master. To give my one hundred (100 %) attention to the person speaking. To try to hear what is said and what is meant, instead of what I think is said and what I believe is meant.

We need to listen to the lips, to hear what is said. Listen to the head, to hear what is meant. Listen to the heart, to hear what is being felt.

We need to listen for the joy, so we can celebrate. Listen for the pain, so that we can respond with care. Listen for the hope, so we can help to keep it alive. Listen for the fear, so that we can bring calm. Listen for the problem so that we can become a part of the solution. Listen for the need to be heard, so that we can give the gift of 'affirming silence.'

We need to Listen with love, it never fails

Know this, my beloved brothers: let every person be quick to hear, slow to speak, slow to anger;
- James 1:19 (ESV)

LIFT OUR CHILDREN AND FAMILIES

Deuteronomy 6:6-7 These commandments that I give you today are to be on your hearts. Impress them on your children. Talk about them when you sit at home and when you walk along the road, when you lie down and when you get up.

1 John 3:2-3 Dear friends, now we are children of God, and what we will be has not yet been made known. But we know that when Christ appears, we shall be like him, for we shall see him as he is. All who have this hope in him purify themselves, just as he is pure.

Joshua 24:15 But if serving the Lord seems undesirable to you, then choose for yourselves this day whom you will serve, whether the gods your ancestors served beyond the Euphrates, or the gods of the Amorites, in whose land you are living. But as for me and my household, we will serve the Lord.

Psalm 127:3-5 Children are a heritage from the Lord, offspring a reward from him. Like arrows in the hands of a warrior are children born in one's youth. Blessed is the man whose quiver is full of them. They will not be put to shame when they contend with their opponents in court.

1 Timothy 3:2-5 Now the overseer is to be above reproach, faithful to his wife, temperate, self-controlled, respectable, hospitable, able to teach, not given to drunkenness, not violent but gentle, not quarrelsome, not a lover of money. He must manage his own family well and see that his children obey him, and he must do so in a manner worthy of full respect. (If anyone does not know how to manage his own family, how can he take care of God's church?)

1 Timothy 5:8 Anyone who does not provide for their relatives, and especially for their own household, has denied the faith and is worse than an unbeliever

Luke 11:13 If you then, though you are evil, know how to give good gifts to your children, how much more will your Father in heaven give the Holy Spirit to those who ask him!

"The Spirit himself bears witness with our spirit that we are children of God, and if children, then heirs, heirs of God and fellow heirs with Christ, provided we suffer with him in order that we may also be glorified with him". - Romans 8:16-17

CHILDREN FIRST

FAMILY FOR BETTER OR WORSE

LOVING OUR CHILDREN

CHILDREN FIRST

The state of our families is one of the major factors affecting the state of our children. Ensuring the welfare and well-being of children is the most important role of the family. On both fronts, there is cause for concern. Not ordinary concern, but grave concern.

Children all over the world, are subject to serious pressures, and exposed to situations and issues that they are not equipped to handle. Many are exposed to violent speech, violent behavior and many times are themselves the victims of violent and abusive behavior. Not only are they the victims of violence from adults, but some are victims of violence committed by other children. The reports in the media, the stories making the rounds and the signs we see around us, are disturbing and are telling us that we are in a crisis.

The same is true for families. The family as an institution and families themselves, are under stress and seem to be coming apart at the seams. Domestic violence is a major cause of death in Jamaica. Women are being beaten, abused in other ways, and killed by their husbands, by the fathers of their children and by men who once declared their 'feelings' for them. Many homes have become "war zones", where words of love and affirmation are rare, even non-existent. Where affection and warmth are strangers, and family members live together as inmates in a common prison, dying for escape, hoping for release.

It is easy to become overwhelmed by the situation. To throw up our hands in despair. To bury our heads in the sand and reminisce on a better time, the good old days . . . when children had manners and adults behaved themselves decently. To stay in our little corner and try to protect our little space. But we cannot survive in 'safe social bubbles'. We have to live in the world. This is the world to which God has called us and in which he has placed us. He calls us to be salt and light in this world, to be examples of what redeemed people are like in this world.

But this is not a battle we can undertake in our own strength, using our own skills and abilities. They are necessary, but they are not equal to the challenge. However we are not alone. We are not without resources. We are not without leadership. As Christians we are under the command of the King of Kings. He knew these days would come and he prayed for us so that we could make a difference and bring hope and life to our dying children and dying families.

Let us recommit ourselves to being agents of spiritual and social transformation. Let us start at home; by being better husbands, wives, fathers, mothers, sons, daughters, aunts, uncles, friends and examples. Rather than curse the darkness let us start to light candles.

Saving the children of the nation and the families of the nation starts with individual action. Each of us must ask ourselves, what can I do to make our children better, make their conditions better, make our families better? Each of us must commit to action and with the grace of God, live out that commitment.

"Preach the Word; be prepared in season and out of season; correct, rebuke and encourage with great patience and careful instruction. For the time will come when men will not put up with sound doctrine, but will gather around them many teachers to say what their itching ears want to hear. They will turn their ears away from the truth and turn aside to myths. But you keep your head in all situations . . . " - 2Timothy 4:2-5 (NIV)

FAMILY FOR BETTER OR WORSE

The family is an important institution. Some would say the most important institution of all. Where there are strong supportive families, there is a greater likelihood that children will become strong, mature and capable individuals, able to cope with the challenges that life will throw at them. Strong families will also produce stronger, more stable societies, as individuals would have learned the values of honesty, respect, mutual care and the discipline of working towards meaningful goals.

Families have always been under pressure from various sources, inside and outside the unit. But these pressures have escalated with time and in some cases, have reached explosive levels. As individuals, the challenges in our families may appear to be overwhelming, and beyond redemption. An unlikely source from which many families grow stronger is adversity. Setbacks and suffering can bring out qualities and inner resources that we never knew we had, for some people and for some families it can make them stronger. But for others it can be devastating, damaging lives and destroying families. Overcoming adversity requires resilience, the ability to 'bounce back.'

We will all face adversity at some time in one form or another.

It is important to understand it and overcome it. Some areas to develop in order to build resilience and equip ourselves and our families to cope better with adversity when it comes, are suggested by noted Jamaican Psychiatrist and Christian, Dr. Anthony Allen as follows:
- Maintaining a positive and adaptive perspective
- Having a moral compass, being guided by a clear sense of right and wrong
- Maintaining a healthy lifestyle, a focus on 'wellness'
- Having cohesive connections in the family
- Experiencing spiritual empowerment
- Being resourceful as individuals and families (if life gives you lemons, make lemonade)

But let us maintain confidence in God's ability to restore that which is broken and play our part in helping our families to be healthy and happy. I invite us to prayerfully reflect on the following passages of Scripture, and to allow God to speak to us through them, as we continue to pray and to put our trust in him, for our families

"The righteous cry, and the Lord hears and delivers them out of all their troubles. The Lord is near to the brokenhearted and saves those who are crushed in spirit. Many are the afflictions of the righteous but the Lord delivers him out of them all. He keeps all his bones, not one of them is broken. Evil shall slay the wicked, and those who hate the righteous will be condemned. The Lord redeems the soul of His servants, and none who take refuge in Him will be condemned." - Psalms 34: 17-22 (NAS)

" The Lord is compassionate and gracious, slow to anger, abounding in love. He will not always accuse, nor will he harbor his anger forever; he does not treat us as our sins deserve or repay us according to our iniquities. For as high as the heavens are above the earth, so great is his love for those who fear him, as far as the

east is from the west so far has he removed our transgressions from us. As a father has compassion on his children so the Lord has compassion on those who fear him; for he knows how we are formed he remembers that we are dust...... But from everlasting to everlasting the Lord's love is with those who fear him, and his righteousness with their children's children. - Psalm 103: 8-17(NIV)

"For this reason, I kneel before the Father. From whom his whole family in heaven and earth derives its name. I pray that out of his glorious riches he may strengthen you with power through his spirit in your inner being..... Now to him who is able to do immeasurably more than all we ask or imagine, according to his great power that is at work within us, to him be glory in the church and in Christ Jesus throughout all generations, for ever and ever! Amen. - Ephesians 4: 14-21 (NIV)

LOVING OUR CHILDREN

It is natural for us as human beings to seek the approval of others. We seek validation of our work and of our worth from those whose opinion matters to us.

Children seek approval from their parents, aunts and uncles, teachers and other adults of influence in their lives. But as they grow, a shift begins to take place, and other persons of influence begin to emerge . . . friends, classmates, cousins, celebrities, movie stars and others in or near their ages, begin to appear to be more important in their lives than their parents or other 'ordinary' adults.

The approval of their peers become seemingly all important. The style of dress, the choice of music, the preferred movies and entertainment, the language, the food, the friends, the ambitions, all have to get the 'well done' from their peers if their life is not to be a total disaster. Many times parents despair and get anxious, because they no longer recognize this child that was so 'nice' when they were small, but now looks and maybe even acts like a stranger.

Some parents try to bridge the gap by trying to become like their children. They learn the language so that they can 'talk the talk.' They get the 'modern makeover,' so they can 'look the look.' They make lifestyle changes, so that they can identify with the younger generation. It is sometimes a sad spectacle that would be laughable if it were not so serious. They want the approval of their children, they want their well done, but as the children would say, duh!

But how do we deal with this shift? How do we cope with this feeling of sometimes being on the outside looking in on the lives of our children? How do we remain authentic and "real" as adults, yet identifying with them, and walking with them through this maze called "growing up"? I am no expert, and upon reflection, perhaps I could have done a better job as a father, but I believe that love is the most critical element in this journey. I love my children (big people) and all children (big and small people).

Love can't be faked. Love is not a technique or a methodology, love is an emotion that motivates and directs our actions. Love helps us to listen, to understand, to console and correct, to make the hard choices, to risk losing their approval now, for their appreciation tomorrow. Love helps us to trust. To trust our children. To affirm them even when they dismiss the affirmation as too much 'fussing over' them, to trust in their possibilities even when they disappoint us and let us down.

Love helps us to trust God. Trust that His strength will make up for our weaknesses and shortcomings, as well as for theirs. Love helps us to pray to him daily for our children. Pray that He would watch over them, and lead them through the treacherous road of life that they sometimes have to travel. Pray that He would draw them to Himself and live His life through them.

A PROMISE FOREVER: HONOUR THY MOTHER AND FATHER

1 John 3:1 "See what kind of love the Father has given to us, that we should be called children of God; and so we are. The reason why the world does not know us is that it did not know him

Proverbs 22:6 Start children off on the way they should go, and even when they are old they will not turn from it.

Proverbs 6:20 My son, keep your father's command and do not forsake your mother's teaching

Proverbs 15:20 A wise son brings joy to his father, but a foolish man despises his mother.

Ephesians 6:4 Fathers, do not exasperate your children; instead, bring them up in the training and instruction of the Lord.

Isaiah 49:15-16 Can a mother forget the baby at her breast and have no compassion on the child she has borne? Though she may forget, I will not forget you! See, I have engraved you on the palms of my hands; your walls are ever before me.

Philippians 4:8 – Finally brethren, whatever is true, whatever is honorable, whatever is just, whatever is pure, whatever is lovely, whatever is of a good report — if there is any virtue and if there is any praise — think on these things.

Proverbs 1:8-9 Listen, my son, to your father's instruction and do not forsake your mother's teaching. They are a garland to grace your head and a chain to adorn your neck.

Deuteronomy 4:9-10 Only be careful, and watch yourselves closely so that you do not forget the things your eyes have seen or let them fade from your heart as long as you live. Teach them to your children and to their children after them. 10 Remember the day you stood before the Lord your God at Horeb, when he said to me, "Assemble the people before me to hear my words so that they may learn to revere me as long as they live in the land and may teach them to their children."

"Children, obey your parents in the Lord, for this is right. "Honor your father and mother" (this is the first commandment with a promise), "that it may go well with you and that you may live long in the land." Fathers, do not provoke your children to anger, but bring them up in the discipline and instruction of the Lord". - Ephesians 6:1-4

THE SPECIAL GIFT OF MOTHERS

GOOD, GOOD FATHER

"ABBA" FATHER

THE SPECIAL GIFT OF MOTHERS

Mothers come in all types. There are quiet, shy and retiring mothers. There are loud, boisterous and aggressive mothers. There are artistic and sophisticated mothers. There are brilliant, academically-gifted mothers. There are hard-driving, business-oriented mothers. There are deeply spiritual, prayer-warrior type mothers. There are fast-paced, hustling-type mothers. There are fashionable, model-type mothers. There are thoughtful, generous and selfless mothers. There are selfish, unkind and harsh mothers. There are mothers who are angels trapped on earth. And then . . . there are mothers who are like devils let loose from hell.

But it is hard to place mothers in categories and types. Most mothers will change their attitudes and actions if the interest of their children requires it. A docile and retiring mother can become a raging warrior if her child is attacked. A poor and financially un-schooled mother can manage her limited finances in ways that would confound the most brilliant financial mind. A mother that is illiterate will stay up with her child doing advanced calculus and nurture that child to one day become an outstanding scientist. A mother, who was into parties and "bling" will give up the "hype" to be a better example to her child. A mother, who grew up without a stable and nurturing home environment, will strive to provide for her child, the emotional security she never got.

Mothers are God's gift to society. It is true that there are many mothers who are terrible and do more harm than good to their children. Mothers who physically and emotionally abandon their children . . . but these mothers are the exceptions.

Most mothers are committed to ensuring that their children are loved, cared for and equipped to thrive in the world. We celebrate those mothers who in these difficult and challenging times provide emotional, material and spiritual support to their children. We also celebrate those mothers who never gave birth themselves, but have nurtured and cared for nieces and nephews, God-children and children unrelated biologically, to them.

I wish for all mothers a very blessed Life. I give thanks to God for my own mother Selma. For the unconditional love, she gave to us her children and the special memories that we each carry with us. I feel blessed to be the husband of a wonderful woman, Faith ("Betty"), who is a great mother to our two children, Stephanie and Sean.

There are many women in the Bible who are wonderful examples of mothers and many passages of Scripture that extol their virtues. One of the most well-known is . . .

"A wife of noble character who can find? She is worth far more than rubies. Her husband has full confidence in her and lacks nothing of value. She brings him good, not harm, all the days of her life. She selects wool and flax and works with eager hands. She is like the merchant ships, bringing her food from afar. She gets up while it is still night; she provides food for her family and portions for her female servants. She considers a field and buys it; out of her earnings she plants a vineyard. She sets about her work vigorously; her arms are strong for her tasks. She sees that her

trading is profitable, and her lamp does not go out at night. In her hand she holds the distaff and grasps the spindle with her fingers. 20 She opens her arms to the poor and extends her hands to the needy. When it snows, she has no fear for her household; for all of them are clothed in scarlet. She makes coverings for her bed; she is clothed in fine linen and purple. Her husband is respected at the city gate, where he takes his seat among the elders of the land. She makes linen garments and sells them, and supplies the merchants with sashes. She is clothed with strength and dignity; she can laugh at the days to come. She speaks with wisdom, and faithful instruction is on her tongue. She watches over the affairs of her household and does not eat the bread of idleness. Her children arise and call her blessed; her husband also, and he praises her: "Many women do noble things, but you surpass them all." Charm is deceptive, and beauty is fleeting; but a woman who fears the LORD is to be praised." - Proverbs 31:10-30

GOOD, GOOD FATHER.

As Christians, we should always be mindful of the importance of praying with persistence. It was based on the account of Jesus' response to His disciples when they asked him to teach them to pray (as John taught his Disciples), as recorded in Luke 11:1-13. In response, He gave them the 'Lord's Prayer.' It was a model, a framework, a guide that they could use in developing their prayer life. Today it is used in worship and repeated in corporate Prayer. But the discourse was more than the provision of a model and guide to praying. Jesus sought to expand their understanding and appreciation of Prayer.

Jesus seemed to have been responding not just to the obvious question of these Disciples, who may have felt somewhat inadequate when they compared themselves to the Disciples of John, but to their deeper need to be able to pray with confidence, conviction and passion. A need we have in common with them.

As He usually did, Jesus used a story to drive home his message. In the story, the friend who had asked for help gave the help, not so much because of the friendship, but because of the need. He then referenced a father's instinct to give to his children what they need and what is good for them, because that is what fathers do. But we are human, our goodness when compared to that of God doesn't even come close. Jesus said: "if you then being evil know how to give good gifts to your children, how much more shall your Father...?"

Some of us have been blessed with great Fathers. My siblings and I have been blessed by the love of a great father, Leslie. Others may not have been so blessed. But Jesus is saying that our heavenly Father's goodness is in a different realm all together. It makes the very best of our human efforts, disposition and goodness, unworthy of mention and incapable of comparison.

I believe Jesus wanted them to understand that Praying is not about a process, a construction of words, or the application of some mystical formula. Prayer is less about who is praying, and more about who they are praying to.

Many times, in our praying we become preoccupied with ourselves. With our fluency. Our ability to quote Scriptures in our praying. In our posture and our phrasing. But we need to remind ourselves that God is not impressed by our efforts. He is touched by our need and He is moved by His love for us.
If we truly understand and appreciate this, then we can say 'Our Father' with a confidence and assurance that will calm our storms, remove our doubts and cocoon us in the warm embrace of our good, good Father.

There's a great song by Chris Tomlin that captures the heart of this relationship.

You're a good, good Father,
It's who You are, it's who You are, it's who you are
And I am loved by You,
It's who I am, it's who I am, it's who I am

Oh, I've heard a thousand stories of what they think you're like
But I've heard the tender whispers of love in the dead of night
And you tell me that you're pleased
And that I'm never alone
You're a Good, Good Father...

Oh, and I've seen many searching for answers far and wide
But I know we're all searching
For answers only you provide
'Cause you know just what we need
Before we say a word
You're a Good, Good Father...

'cause you are perfect in all of your ways
You are perfect in all of your ways
You are perfect in all of your ways to us
You're a Good, Good Father...

Oh, it's love so undeniable
I, I can hardly speak
Peace so unexplainable
I, I can hardly think
You're a Good, Good Father...

"ABBA" FATHER

"Honour thy father and thy mother. . ." This is the fifth of the Ten Commandments and the first that ends with a promise. A promise with the conditionality that if you honor your father and mother,

". . . *you may live long in the land the Lord your God is giving you*" - Exodus 20:12.

This Commandment of God, is generally regarded by most societies, regardless of religious belief, as a moral imperative, brooking no opposition. As Christians, however, it is a Commandment, as with all the other Commandments, that transcends mere "moral imperative", to an absolute "written in stone" directive from the most "High God, Creator of heaven and earth", our Father. A directive that we who are children of God, must obey, and by so doing, fulfill our purpose, which is to glorify him. "Children, obey your parents in the Lord, for this is right. Honor your father and mother which is the first commandment with a promise, so that it may be well with you, and that you may live long on the earth" - Ephesians 6:1-3

All of us as Children of God have all been disobedient, "for all have sinned and fall short of the glory of God" - Romans 3:23. We are blessed however to have a loving Father, one who "If we confess our sins, he is faithful and just and will forgive us our sins and purify us from all unrighteousness" – 1 John 1:9. A Father whom the Psalmist declares "Just as a father has compassion on his children, So the LORD has compassion on those who fear Him" - Psalm 103:13.

We who embrace God as our Father and His divine acknowledgement of us as his children " . . . And I will be your Father, and you will be my sons and daughters, says the Lord Almighty" - 2 Corinthians 6:18, must strive to worship him in spirit and in truth, in thoughts, words and deeds, knowing that His word is sure " . . . those who honor Me; I will honor, and those who despise Me shall be lightly esteemed" - 1 Samuel 2:30.

As we journey through life, we should therefore always be mindful, that our God, our "Abba" (the Hebrew word for Father) is "ever present, ever faithful, ever sure", and it is our duty as his children, to yield, in humble submission, to his authority and honour him. " . . . yet for us there is but one God, the Father, from whom are all things and we exist for Him; and one Lord, Jesus Christ, by whom are all things, and we exist through Him - 1 Corinthians 8:6
To you Father, we give all honour and praise and pray continually for your mercy and blessing, as you have taught us, through your Son Jesus Christ:

Our Father which art in heaven, Hallowed be thy name
Thy kingdom come, Thy will be done in earth as it is in heaven
Give us this day our daily bread, And forgive us our debts, as we forgive our debtors
And lead us not into temptation, but deliver us from evil
For thine is the kingdom, and the power, and the glory, forever, Amen - Matthew 6:9-13

BEHOLD THE LORD GOD

Comfort ye, comfort ye my people, saith your God.

Speak ye comfortably to Jerusalem, and cry unto her, that her warfare is accomplished, that her iniquity is pardoned: for she hath received of the LORD's hand double for all her sins

The voice of him that crieth in the wilderness, Prepare ye the way of the LORD, make straight in the desert a highway for our God

Every valley shall be exalted, and every mountain and hill shall be made low: and the crooked shall be made straight, and the rough places plain

And the glory of the LORD shall be revealed, and all flesh shall see it together: for the mouth of the LORD hath spoken it

The voice said, Cry. And he said, What shall I cry?

All flesh is grass, and all the goodliness thereof is as the flower of the field: The grass withereth, the flower fadeth: because the spirit of the LORD bloweth upon it: surely the people is grass. The grass withereth, the flower fadeth: but the word of our God shall stand for ever.

O Zion, that bringest good tidings, get thee up into the high mountain; O Jerusalem, that bringest good tidings, lift up thy voice with strength; lift it up, be not afraid; say unto the cities of Judah, Behold your God!

Behold, the Lord GOD will come with strong hand, and his arm shall rule for him: behold, his reward is with him, and his work before him.

He shall feed his flock like a shepherd: he shall gather the lambs with his arm, and carry them in his bosom, and shall gently lead those that are with young [Isaiah 40:1-11 KJV]

And the Word became flesh and dwelt among us, and we have seen his glory, glory as of the only Son from the Father, full of grace and truth - John 1:14

———————————

GOOD NEWS! GREAT JOY!

JOY BEYOND CHRISTMAS

THE PRESENT OF PRESENCE

GOOD NEWS! GREAT JOY!

The story of Christmas has challenged and inspired mankind for centuries. It brings together an unlikely cast of characters, to provide color and texture to a story that is filled with the awesomeness of the divine, and the ordinariness of the human.

Wise men from the East endure the hazards and difficulties of traveling hundreds of miles to see the Baby Jesus, whilst Herod the King was totally ignorant of his arrival. The Religious Leaders who had studied the prophecies about the coming Messiah, and who thought they knew all the signs of his arrival, missed it completely, whilst humble, unschooled Shepherds, got a royal invitation to witness the divine historic moment.

It is a story that has inspired many books, poems, plays, songs, movies and messages. Even though it's a story that is centuries old and is one of the most well known in history, it continues throughout the ages, to remain current, to attract attention, to inspire people and to impact lives.

It is a story that is many sided and many layered. It engages the intellectual in their search for knowledge and understanding. It engages the religious in their search for truth. It engages ordinary people in its simple yet powerful illustration of God's love and His interest and involvement in the lives of ordinary people.

The shepherds were the "ordinariest" of the ordinary. They were introduced to us as "some shepherds living out in the field." No names were given, no great description, not even where they were living was identified, just some shepherds living somewhere. Yet their ordinariness was about to be transformed by a 'heavenly visitation".

"And an angel of the Lord suddenly stood before them, and the glory of the Lord shone round about them; and they were terribly frightened. But the angel said to them, "do not be afraid, for behold I bring you good news of great joy which shall be for all people; for today in the city of David has been born for you a Savior, who is Christ the Lord."- Luke2:9-10 (NAS)

Yes, in this unnamed place, to these unnamed shepherds, leading ordinary and for the most part, uneventful lives, came a message that bent the arc of history and changed the future of man forever. A message with life-changing significance, that was both personal to them and universal to mankind.
The Saviour, your Saviour, the Saviour of mankind is born.

The story of Christmas is the story of the Wise men from the East, of Herod the hostile King, of a people waiting for their Messiah, but so caught up in the busy-ness of life, not to notice his arrival. It is a story of two parents who could not find a decent room in which to have their baby delivered. It is the story of a baby who was destined to change the world, having a manger for his crib. It is a story of some unknown shepherds who heard the news first and were obedient to the call, and was among the first to worship Him.

The shepherds returned to their unnamed place and their ordinary lives, but they went, "glorifying and praising God for all that they had heard and seen." I pray that for each of us, just like the shepherds, the story of Christmas will inspire us to engage in the process of discovering or rediscovering in a deeply personal way, this 'good news of great joy.'

JOY BEYOND CHRISTMAS

The season of Christmas is one of the most joyous periods in the world. For us as Christians it has special significance and great meaning. Our celebration is grounded in the understanding that the event we celebrate represents the critical turning point in human history.

The story of Christmas, is the story of God choosing to send His son Jesus, 'to walk in our shoes.' As the Apostle John wrote: "And the Word became flesh and dwelt among us . . . .full of grace and truth.". It is the story of a loving God expressing that love, by giving that which was most precious to Him, his only son to enter the world of mankind, and through Him, bring redemption to a lost world. The circumstance of his birth and the humble life that he lived demonstrates the inclusiveness of that love.

The message of Christmas is the message that God so loved us, that He sent His son to be one of us. Not to go 'undercover", or to wear a body suit for a few days, and then return to his throne, but to live his life as a human being, and to end it with a painful death. For Him it was not an act. It was not a reality show. It was an expression of divine love as expressed in John 3:16: "For God so loved the world that He gave his only begotten son that whosoever believeth in Him, should not perish, but have everlasting life."

The Christmas season has its share of controversy about the accuracy of the date, the pagan origin of the festival and the increasingly commercialized nature of Christmas. These issues however, should not rob us as Christians of celebrating 'Our Christmas'. Christmas is a time of joy. The shepherds rejoiced when they visited the baby. The Wise men 'rejoiced with exceedingly great joy' when they found the baby. The angel declared " I bring you good tidings of great joy."

Life is hard and sometimes the going gets very rough. If we are not careful, we focus so much on the hardship and challenges, that we do not take time to experience the joy of living. To celebrate the many people and things in our lives that have enriched our journey and make us uniquely who we are. To unscrew the face and open the heart. To let go of some burdens that we have made the controllers in our lives. To relax and know that God is not 'off duty' and He does not mind giving you time to laugh, to have fun, to experience joy.

At that time Mary got ready and hurried to a town in the hill country of Judea, where she entered Zechariah's home and greeted Elizabeth. When Elizabeth heard Mary's greeting, the baby leaped in her womb, and Elizabeth was filled with the Holy Spirit. In a loud voice, she exclaimed: "Blessed are you among women, and blessed is the child you will bear! But why am I so favored, that the mother of my Lord should come to me? As soon as the sound of your greeting reached my ears, the baby in my womb leaped for joy. Blessed is she who has believed that what the Lord has said to her will be accomplished!" - Luke 1:39-45 (KJV)

THE PRESENT OF PRESENCE

One of the most common features of the celebration of Christmas is the giving and receiving of gifts.
For some persons, it is the receiving of gifts that makes the season special. If the gift does not live up to expectation, the giver falls in ranking as a relative or friend, or falls off the ranking completely.

Most of us can remember some childhood gift that 'hit the spot' in our own childhood imaginations. At the time, our world was perfect because our Christmas presents brightened up our lives and brought excitement and joy to our world.

On the first Christmas, Baby Jesus also got presents. They were not exactly what we imagine a child would dream of, or even appreciate. Which little child would get excited about gold, much less frankincense and myrrh? But inappropriate though they may seem, they were given with much thought and each item had its significance.

The truth is that gifts are a form of communicating. They carry a message. They say something about the giver, about the receiver and about their relationship. Sometimes there are constraints affecting the giver and they are unable to give the gift they really want. But it is up to the receiver to see beyond the tangible gift, to the sentiment, emotion and thought behind it.

Sometimes the seemingly least expensive gift, is the most valuable, because what it may lack in cost, is more than made up for in heart. There is an art to giving. But I believe there is an even finer art to receiving. The art of gratitude, the art of allowing the giver to be enriched in their giving, where the attention is more on the presence than the presents.

Presents without presence are mere products. They may have utility value, but they do not move the emotional dial. Yet presence is highly underrated. We tend to take it for granted. After all, we cannot buy it in a gift shop or boutique, no fine jeweler has it in a showcase and it cannot be packaged or gift wrapped.

Presence is about being there for someone, giving our one hundred percent (100%). Our attention, our focus, our time, our care, our love, our whole being. It is about where we choose to be, in mind, heart and body. It is so easy to give things. Perhaps too, it may be easy to give time. But, to give our presence takes effort. It is about what is important to us in the given moment.

I pray that even as our Christian generosity of spirit leads us to give presents, beyond Christmas and all year 'round, that we give what is truly priceless, the gift of presence, in Jesus's name. Amen.

And Mary said: *"My soul glorifies the Lord and my spirit rejoices in God my Savior, for he has been mindful of the humble state of his servant. From now on all generations will call me blessed, for the Mighty One has done great things for me—holy is his name. His mercy extends to those who fear him, from generation to generation. He has performed mighty deeds with his arm; He has scattered those who are proud in their inmost thoughts. He has brought down rulers from their thrones but has lifted up the humble. He has filled the hungry with good things but has sent the rich away empty. He has helped his servant Israel, remembering to be merciful to Abraham and his descendants forever, even as he said to our fathers."* - Luke 1:46-55 KJV

ALL WE NEED FOR CHRISTMAS IS EMMANUEL

The observation of Christmas, a tradition celebrated in many forms, across the world, is, at its core, a festival that is used to mark the Anniversary of the birth of Jesus Christ, bringing with it, the message of joy, hope and redemption that his birth signifies.

The observance of Christmas varies from culture to culture and from country to country. These differences reflect the ways in which societies have wrapped Christmas with their own traditions, practices and lifestyles. In some cases this 'wrapping' has been so overwhelming, that the message of Christmas is completely lost. People immerse themselves in the commercial and festive "feel good" whirlpool of shopping, eating, drinking, partying and other pleasurable indulgencies. For many persons, the only relationship they acknowledge between Christmas and the Christ of Christmas is that the word Christ is found in Christmas.

We need to escape from the noisy allure of the 'Christmas market' calling us to buy this and buy that, offering deals of a lifetime, and discounts you will never see again. We need to escape from the pressing crowds, going nowhere, weaving their way through streets and shops, a swirling mass of humanity searching for that elusive basket of goods that will make this

Christmas magical. We need to escape from the voices around us and in us that suggest that new paint, new clothes, new furniture, new linen, new this and new that, will bring us Christmas joys beyond compare.

The Christ we celebrate, chose to be born in the most humble of settings, without many of the human comforts one would have expected. Born in settings far removed from the prestige and luxury associated with the birth of a king, much less the King of Kings. His birth brought with it a simple message: "Fear not because I bring you good tidings of great joy which shall be to all people, for unto you is born this day, in the city of David, a saviour who is Christ the Lord.

Let us escape from the Christmas man has created, with its overpowering culture of consumption and rediscover the Christmas God initiated. A time of peace and goodwill to all men. A time to enjoy the greatest gift of all, the gift of Emanuel, God with us.

O come, O come, Emmanuel
And ransom captive Israel
That mourns in lonely exile here
Until the Son of God appear
Rejoice! Rejoice! Emmanuel
Shall come to thee, O Israel.

O come, Thou Rod of Jesse, free
Thine own from Satan's tyranny
From depths of Hell Thy people save
And give them victory o'er the grave
Rejoice! Rejoice! Emmanuel
Shall come to thee, O Israel.

O come, Thou Day-Spring, come and cheer

Our spirits by Thine advent here
Disperse the gloomy clouds of night
And death's dark shadows put to flight.
Rejoice! Rejoice! Emmanuel
Shall come to thee, O Israel.
O come, Thou Key of David, come,
And open wide our heavenly home;
Make safe the way that leads on high,
And close the path to misery.
Rejoice! Rejoice! Emmanuel
Shall come to thee, O Israel.

O come, O come, Thou Lord of might,
Who to Thy tribes, on Sinai's height,
In ancient times did'st give the Law,
In cloud, and majesty and awe.
Rejoice! Rejoice! Emmanuel
Shall come to thee, O Israel

[Originally written in Latin text in the 12th Century, by Author and Composer unknown. The Latin was translated into English by John Mason Neale in 1851]

I KNOW THAT MY REDEEMER LIVES

1 Corinthians 15:3-5 Christ died for our sins according to the Scriptures, that he was buried, that he was raised on the third day

Romans 6:9 We know that Christ, being raised from the dead, will never die again; death no longer has dominion over him

Romans 4:25 He was delivered up for our trespasses and raised for our justification

1 Peter 1:3 According to his great mercy, he has caused us to be born again to a living hope through the resurrection of Jesus Christ from the dead

Romans 6:4 ...just as Christ was raised from the dead by the glory of the Father, we too might walk in newness of life.

Romans 6:5 For if we have been united with him in a death like his, we shall certainly be united with him in a resurrection like his

John 11:25-26 I am the resurrection and the life. Whoever believes in me, though he die, yet shall he live, and everyone who lives and believes in me shall never die. Do you believe this?

Romans 8:11 If the Spirit of him who raised Jesus from the dead dwells in you, he who raised Christ Jesus from the dead will also give life to your mortal bodies through his Spirit who dwells in you.

Job 19:25 As for me, I know that my Redeemer lives, and at the last He will take His stand on the earth

"Praise be to the God and Father of our Lord Jesus Christ! In his great mercy he has given us new birth into a living hope through the resurrection of Jesus Christ from the dead." - 1 Peter 1:3

LIFE AMAZING!

WISDOM IN OUR WILDERNESS

SOMETHING SPECIAL ABOUT HIM

HE'S STANDING IN THE RING WITH YOU

LIFE AMAZING!

Life is the most precious gift that we have as human beings. Without it all other gifts lose their value. One may even say that without it no other gift can be given, received, much less can be enjoyed. Yet it is a gift that is often taken for granted, unrecognized, uncelebrated and unappreciated.

The Easter story, is a celebration of life and a reminder of its preciousness. It is also a reminder of the source of life and the purpose of life. By bringing Jesus back to life from the cruel death by crucifixion, God demonstrated that He is the Lord of life. He gives life, he allows life to be taken away and he can restore life. God is the source of life, he breathed into man and man became a living soul.

The resurrection also allowed the life of Jesus to glorify and bring honour to His Father. The purpose of life is to glorify God, the giver of life. This precious gift that He has given to each of us, comes with an expectation that we will use it in a way that honors Him, and brings glory to His name.

Easter is a time of drama, it celebrates one of the most earth shattering events of history. It marks the triumph of Jesus Christ over Satan and his forces that sought to keep the world captive to sin. It marks the triumph of good over evil, of love over hate and of life over death. It opened the way to our redemption and to a new life. A life lived for the glory of God, through the power of God, because of the love of God.

I invite us to reflect on the message of Easter, and to draw strength from the promise of Easter. Strength to overcome the 'life robbers' in ourselves and around us, those situations and forces that take away from the richness and the joy that God has provided, in His gift of life. A gift freely and fully given to you and to me.

Let us live with 'grateful amazement.' Amazement that He loves us. Amazement that He cares. Amazement that He died for us. Amazement that He was resurrected for us. Amazement that we can receive new life in Him. Amazement that regardless of who we are, and what our circumstances are, we can live amazing lives through this amazing God who is alive in our hearts.

"According to his great mercy, he has caused us to be born again to a living hope through the resurrection of Jesus Christ from the dead". - 1 Peter 1:3

WISDOM IN OUR WILDERNESS

In the period of Lent, Christians reflect on the experience of Jesus as he spent forty days and forty nights in the wilderness. Many of us use this time as an opportunity to practice acts of self-denial aimed at leading us to focus more attention on spiritual things. This is a worthy effort and if pursued for the right reason and which, with the right attitude, will enhance one's Christian walk.

One of the lessons we can learn is the importance of being sensitive to the Spirit of God. We are told that Jesus was "led of the Spirit, into the wilderness." To be in a position to be led, requires that one must be in a position to hear. In St. John 10:27 we are told: "my sheep hear my voice and, I know them and they follow me." If we allow ourselves to be distracted by the noises around us, legitimate and useful though they may be, we may not be able to clearly hear the Spirit speaking to us and thereby miss His leading.

Another lesson, is the lesson of obedience. There is no indication that Jesus protested in any way, or displayed any reluctance to follow the leading of the Spirit. In the Garden of Gethsemane, he left the decision to his Father. He went willingly into this forsaken place, because that was where he was being sent, by his Father.

There is also the lesson of endurance. One night in the wilderness, even a week possibly, might have been tolerable, but forty days and forty nights was a true test of endurance. He had no food, no creature comforts, no company, no prayer partners, no CDs or iPod with inspiring music to lift the spirit, no Bible to read for instruction and spiritual strength. He was on his own and alone. It was a hard test, but he endured and overcame.

Another lesson is the lesson of reliance on the Word. At the end of the period was the big test, the finals, the showdown. The devil did not send some low-level demon to tempt Jesus, this was too important a mission. This was a high-stake battle. He had to pull out the big guns. He had to handle this himself. He had been preparing for this day and had centuries of experience. He was smart, cunning, skillful and focused. He had deceived many before and expected that in this desolate place, he would have his greatest victory. But Jesus was prepared. He had 'hidden the Word of God in his heart'. He was ready.

Like David facing Goliath, Jesus resorted to his weapon of choice. For David it was the sling, for Jesus it was the Word of God. When Satan sent his first missile, Jesus shot it down with a weapon, powerful in it's simplicity, he responded: "IT IS WRITTEN."

As we face our wildernesses, and our temptations, let us learn from the master and face them with faith. Jesus showed us how. He has given us His Spirit and His Word. He has invested in our success.

"Thy word have I hid in my heart, that I might not sin against you." - Psalm 119:11(KJV)

SOMETHING SPECIAL ABOUT HIM

On Palm Sunday, Christians across the world are being reminded of Jesus' triumphal entry into Jerusalem. He was surrounded by adoring men, women and children, straining to get a glimpse of this great person whose words had electrified audiences, whose actions had brought healing and deliverance to people wherever he went, and whose presence gave hope and inspiration to thousands.

As they joined the throngs of persons winding their way along the journey, each person must have been privately wondering to themselves if he was the 'Promised One' . . . the 'Anointed One?" . . . the Messiah". They must have been wondering to themselves if this is the dawning of a new day . . . Can we begin to hope again? Is God finally hearing our cry? will he finally break the yoke of our oppressors?

But as they got closer and got a glimpse of him, small seeds of doubt must have begun to creep into their minds. If he is the liberator, where is his army, where are the mighty warriors, where are the weapons of war? Who are these bunch of stragglers close to him? They looked more like fishermen than soldiers. Where was his horse? Surely the King of the Jews should be riding in majestically, on a powerful steed, towering over the crowd and projecting an aura of power and royal majesty.

Instead he was seated on the back of a donkey, without the trappings of royalty and seemingly unaffected by the 'crowd of fans' marching with him. But there was something about him that was clear to all around, this was no ordinary man, there was something unique about him, something divine.

He was truly unique, he was a king like no other before him and no other since. He did not need an army. He did not need an earthly throne. He did not need the approval of men or the sanction of rulers. His path to his throne was through suffering and death, and through his death and resurrection, he would bring eternal life to mankind.

"As they were untying the colt, its owners asked them, why are you untying the colt? They replied, the Lord needs it. They brought it to Jesus, threw their cloaks on the colt and put Jesus on it. As he went along, people spread their cloaks on the road. When he came near where the road goes down the Mount of Olives, the whole crowd began joyfully to praise God in loud voices for all the miracles they had seen: Blessed is the king who comes in the name of the Lord! Peace in heaven and glory in the highest." -St. Luke 20: 36- 37 (NIV)

HE'S STANDING IN THE RING WITH YOU

The celebration of Easter is a celebration of life and a celebration of hope. It is the vivid contrast between the darkness and despair of the Crucifixion, and the brilliance and hope of the Resurrection. In the short time between the Crucifixion and the Resurrection, the ultimate struggle between good and evil, between God and his archenemy Satan is played out. It was the fight of the ages, a war for the souls of men and the future of the world.

In the ring were Satan and his army of evil. Men and women blinded by his lies, seduced by his various enticements and mindlessly following his bidding. They had no idea of the bigger war going on. A war in which they were mere pawns being used as by Satan to give Jesus the 'knock out' punch.

But also in the ring was Jesus, the Messiah, the Prince of Peace, and the Son of God seemingly alone in His corner. His crowd had deserted him. Fleeing in fear and despair. His closest associates had abandoned Him, denying knowledge of Him and watching from afar as the one they claimed to love and follow was condemned to suffer and die. In the ring, he did not look triumphant. He did not look like a champion in the making. He was not to be cheered in victory. He was to be mocked and jeered as a pathetic "loser".

Destroying the Son of God was Satan's mission and passion. For him there was no greater cause. It was a popular cause. The crowds were with him. In their eyes, Satan in his various disguises was the undisputed champion and he wore the heavy-weight crown. The crowds urged him on with their bloodthirsty shouts of Crucify Him! Crucify Him! He could taste the victory... and there you have it!... BAMMM!... the courts ruled in his favor and Pilate handed out his judgement... Jesus will be crucified! In mock salute to his "defeat", they placed the title 'King of the Jews' above his head, on the cross of His crucifixion.

This Jesus, He who had healed many people of their sicknesses; given back sight to the blind; opened the mouths of those who were dumb; and made the crippled able to walk again. Thousands had been fed by him, and thousands had been inspired and uplifted by His words. This Jesus now stood alone; abandoned, rejected, ridiculed, beaten, battered, bruised, disfigured and despised.

But Jesus's life could not end on a cross. He could not be held in a grave. His mission could not be stopped by Satan and his band of evil men. God alone is the Author and finisher of our fate. God alone "run things", not Satan. He alone could send his only begotten son to live, be crucified, and rise from the grave as our Redeemer, Saviour and Lord. He is risen! He Lives! Our God reigns!

At Calvary, Satan thought he had won. But Jesus alone knew the game plan. He knew that his victory was through the painful portal of seeming defeat. He knew that there was power in his "blood" and new life in his Resurrection. The tomb that Satan thought would have sealed and secured his victory, would become the portal through which the risen Christ would proclaim His indisputable power and glory as the Son of God, and Savior of the world.

We all have our time in the ring, our epic battles and life-threatening struggles. But regardless of what the enemy and his forces are up to in the ring, or what he is trying to do to us, our Risen Lord stands with us. He is our guarantee of victory over defeat. Of hope over despair. Of life over death. Because He overcame, so can we. Because He lives, so will we.

"Jesus said unto her, I am the resurrection and the life: He that believeth in me, though he were dead, yet shall he live: and whosoever liveth and believeth in me shall never die. Believest thou this?" - St. John 11: 25-26 (KJV)

THE PARABLE OF THE PRODIGAL SON

And he said, "There was a man who had two sons. And the younger of them said to his father, 'Father, give me the share of property that is coming to me.' And he divided his property between them. Not many days later, the younger son gathered all he had and took a journey into a far country, and there he squandered his property in reckless living. And when he had spent everything, a severe famine arose in that country, and he began to be in need. So he went and hired himself out to[a] one of the citizens of that country, who sent him into his fields to feed pigs. And he was longing to be fed with the pods that the pigs ate, and no one gave him anything.

"But when he came to himself, he said, 'How many of my father's hired servants have more than enough bread, but I perish here with hunger! I will rise and go to my father, and I will say to him, "Father, I have sinned against heaven and before you. I am no longer worthy to be called your son. Treat me as one of your hired servants."' And he arose and came to his father. But while he was still a long way off, his father saw him and felt compassion, and ran and embraced him and kissed him. And the son said to him, 'Father, I have sinned against heaven and before you. I am no longer worthy to be called your son.'[b] But the father said to his servants,[c] 'Bring quickly the best robe, and put it on him, and put a ring on his hand, and shoes on his feet. And bring the fattened calf and kill it, and let us eat and celebrate. For this my son was dead, and is alive again; he was lost, and is found.' And they began to celebrate.

"Now his older son was in the field, and as he came and drew near to the house, he heard music and dancing. 26 And he called one of the servants and asked what these things meant. And he said to him, 'Your brother has come, and your father has killed the fattened calf, because he has received him back safe and sound.' But he was angry and refused to go in. His father came out and entreated him, but he answered his father, 'Look, these many years I have served you, and I never disobeyed your command, yet you never gave me a young goat, that I might celebrate with my friends. But when this son of yours came, who has devoured your property with prostitutes, you killed the fattened calf for him!' And he said to him, 'Son, you are always with me, and all that is mine is yours. It was fitting to celebrate and be glad, for this your brother was dead, and is alive; he was lost, and is found." - Luke 15:11-32 ESV

"Live as people who are free, not using your freedom as a cover-up for evil, but living as servants of God. Honor everyone. Love the brotherhood. Fear God. Honor the emperor." – 1 Peter 2:16-17

THE ILLUSION OF INDEPENDENCE

MAXIMIZE THE MOMENT

FREE TO CHOOSE

THE ILLUSION OF INDEPENDENCE

Mankind has an innate desire for independence. To be free from external controls and restrictions. To be the captain of one's ship. To call the shots in one's life. To be able to say "I did it my way".

The process of growth is a gradual acquisition of independence. Each phase comes with new freedoms. As mastery is shown, new doors are opened until one day you get the "keys". Society assumes that this process has an age criteria and so there is a 'coming of age.'

But independence comes with a pair of twins, 'opportunity and responsibility.' They are inseparable, and for many this is a painful discovery. The new car has to be maintained, the new apartment has to be furnished, the new baby has to be cared for. New words enter the vocabulary; rent, light bill, taxes, mortgage, doctor bill, 'bruk' pocket, etc.

When we see only one of the twins, when we only see the opportunity and the options, and not the responsibilities and consequences, what we have is the 'illusion of Independence'. The "appearance" of freedom, but we are "blind" to the hidden chains that bind, or the hidden weights that will sink the ship.

The story of the Prodigal Son is a story that describes one young man's search for independence, and the rocky road that took him on the red carpet to ruin. He had come of age. He wanted his independence and he grabbed it. He held his dreams in his hands. Nothing stood between him and the life he wanted. He had it all planned. He had imagined and dreamed about this new life, and now it was here, and he had the means to experience it without constraint.

He was young, healthy and wealthy. He only needed distance between himself and the old boring life. He wanted as much space, as possible between him and the restricted life of his youth. But he would soon discover that leaving home did not guarantee independence. He would soon come to know that he would pay a price for his "youthful exuberance". But his father was always in the background. For even though his journey would be rough and painful rejection of all his father stood for and valued, his father's love remained unchanged and would ultimately rescue him from himself.

He discovered that the journey he was on, only gave him the illusion of independence, that true independence would need a change of heart, change of mind and a change of direction. I invite you to reflect on the journey of the prodigal, because in some way or the other, each of us has a "prodigal story" and its lesson of hope still inspires us today.

MAXIMIZE THE MOMENT

Jeremiah 29:11 is a well-known passage and has been a source of encouragement to many people, especially in times of difficulty and uncertainty. Dr. Tony Evans asserted in one of his online sermons, that it is a "great Verse in a bad Chapter". He elaborated on the dire circumstances in which the Children of Israel had found themselves.

They were in exile in Babylon, removed from the familiarity, comfort and security of their native land. They were in a place of foreign gods and foreign practices. They were there as punishment for their unfaithfulness to God and were estranged from Him. Their situation was aggravated by false prophets who were telling them that their condition would soon change. That in a short time they would be free to return to their homeland and to a more peaceful and prosperous life.

Jeremiah's message from God shattered this false hope that was being created. They would not be returning home soon. In fact, they would be spending another seventy (70) years in exile. On the surface, this was very bad news and must have caused great anxiety and discouragement among the people. But there was more to the message than about the length of their stay. God also gave them instruction about what they should do. They should settle down and live productive lives in the land of exile.

Dr. Evans used a term that I found very instructive, he said that they were being told to 'maximize the moment.' This term is relevant to us regardless of our circumstances. In good times or in bad, at home or abroad, in freedom or captivity, we are called to maximize the moment. To occupy till He comes. To do everything heartily as unto God.

Yes, if our situation is not good and we want to see changes, we should pray ardently for God to bring about the changes we desire. We should however be productive while we wait. We should make the best of the resources and opportunities that we have, even if they are not what we would have preferred. We should maximize the moment.

Even though the situation may look like God has abandoned us to the "Babylonians", He has not. He is with us in our 'Babylon' and sends His word to remind us, that He has a plan for us. Armed with this knowledge we can learn to 'maximize our moments' till freedom come and beyond . . .

"Build houses and settle down. Plant gardens and eat what you grow in them. Marry and have children. Then let your children get married, so that they also may have children. You must increase in numbers and not decrease. Work for the good of the cities where I have made you prisoners...... I alone know the plans I have for you, plans to bring you prosperity and not disaster, plans to bring about the future you hope for. Then you will call to me. You will come and pray to me, and I will answer you. You will seek me, and you will find me, because you will seek me with all your heart."
- Jeremiah 29:5-13 (TEV)

FREE TO CHOOSE

A culture of gratitude greatly enriches the human experience. When last have you stopped to give thanks for the positive things about your country, the positive things about your community, the positive things about your church, the positive things about your family, or the positive things about yourself?

For many of us, when we wake up each morning, the privilege of our geographic location, and socio-political realities, allow us to face the day as free people, living in a free country, governed by laws, with checks and balances in the system.

We are free to associate with whomever we choose. We are free, within reason, to do whatever we want to do, or free to say what we want to say, when we want to say it, and where we want to say it. We are free to move around the country, without "Passes" or permission to travel from one place to another. We are free to choose leaders, to criticize, commend or laugh at them. We are free to worship whom we choose, when we choose and how we choose. We are free to buy what we want, where we want and when we want as our resources allow. We are free to marry whom we choose (within the law), have children and raise our families as we choose.

It is easy to take our freedoms for granted. To forget that for many people around the world today, freedom is not a reality. We are in a time when some people are still treated as property, to be bought and sold, traded like animals and sometimes treated worse than them. A time when political leaders are imposed upon the people against their will and they have no vote and no voice. A time when acquiring an education and achieving material and professional success is an "idle dream".

But even in those 'freedom less' places, there are people emancipated by their faith, though imprisoned by men. People for whom prisons are powerless and chains meaningless. People who resist religious oppression and choose praise in spite of persecution.

I am challenged by them as I challenge you, to embrace freedom, to choose to live as free persons. To recognize that the chains that bind us are often of our own creation. The bars that imprison us are often the fears we ourselves cultivate. The limits we face, are so often the ones we impose upon ourselves.

We are blessed with the freedom to choose. The freedom to choose good over evil. To choose love over hate. To choose peace over war. To choose to give rather than always to get. To choose to serve rather than to be served. To choose to live rather than exist. To choose God instead of mammon. To choose to express always the beauty of Jesus in an increasingly coarse and ugly world enabled by the gift and grace of Jesus the Liberator.

Christianity is about freedom. Freedom from the power of sin and freedom to become what God designed us to be. The Apostle Paul reminds us: *"It was for freedom that Christ set us free, stand firm then, and do not be burdened again by a yoke of slavery."* - Galatians 5:1 (NIV)

INCREASE THE FRUITS OF YOUR RIGHTEOUSNESS

Psalm 31:19-20 How abundant are the good things that you have stored up for those who fear you, that you bestow in the sight of all, on those who take refuge in you. In the shelter of your presence you hide them from all human intrigues; you keep them safe in your dwelling from accusing tongues.

2 Corinthians 9:10 Now He who supplies seed to the sower and bread for food will supply and multiply your seed for sowing and increase the harvest of your righteousness;

Luke 6:38 - Give, and it shall be given unto you; good measure, pressed down, and shaken together, and running over, shall men give into your bosom. For with the same measure that ye mete withal it shall be measured to you again

Acts 20:35 - I have shewed you all things, how that so labouring ye ought to support the weak, and to remember the words of the Lord Jesus, how he said, It is more blessed to give than to receive.

1 John 3:17 - But whoso hath this world's good, and seeth his brother have need, and shutteth up his bowels of compassion from him, how dwelleth the love of God in him?

2 Corinthians 9:6 - But this I say, He which soweth sparingly shall reap also sparingly; and he which soweth bountifully shall reap also bountifully.

Matthew 9:37 Then He said to His disciples, The harvest is plentiful, but the workers are few.

Psalm 107:1,8-9 Give thanks to the LORD, for he is good; his love endures forever. Let them give thanks to the Lord for his unfailing love and his wonderful deeds for mankind, for he satisfies the thirsty and fills the hungry with good things

Matthew 9:37 Then He said to His disciples, The harvest is plentiful, but the workers are few.

"Do not be deceived, my beloved brothers. Every good gift and every perfect gift is from above, coming down from the Father of lights, with whom there is no variation or shadow due to change. Of his own will he brought us forth by the word of truth, that we should be a kind of first fruits of his creatures". - James 1:16-18

HONOUR GOD'S HARVEST WITH OUR BEST

GIVING FROM 'BORROWED GOODS.'

THE RHYTHM OF THE SEASONS OF LIFE

HONOUR GOD'S HARVEST WITH OUR BEST

As a child, growing up in rural Jamaica, I looked forward to my church's Harvest. It was a time of celebration and there was an air of great excitement about it. On the Saturday before, there would be a steady stream of persons bringing their gifts for Harvest. Donkeys with their hampers laden with ground provisions would be carefully 'parked' in the church yard and their goods unloaded. Children scurrying in with bags and baskets of all types, filled with a variety of fruits and / or vegetables. Men and women struggling with huge bunches of bananas, baskets with corn, yams, sweet potato and other crops in season.

The Saturday night was the big preparation. Towering sugar cane, their leaves intact, were usually placed in bundles to stand in the corners of the church, like reverent watchmen. At the front of the church, all manner of produce were positioned for visual effect . . . bunches of bananas, stacked upright; mounds of yams, with pride of place going to the larger tubers; ears of corn and bundles of carrots, along with containers of tomatoes, brought colour to the displays. Coco and dasheen sometimes made it through, but in those days, they were held in low esteem. There was also the 'agro-products' of chocolate, coconut drops, corn pone, potato pudding, gizzadas, along with other items like eggs, ripe banana, coconut and oranges.

Sometimes there were 'live gifts' such as hens (chicken) and roosters and the occasional goat.

Then there was the market day, with intense haggling over prices and friendly banter of whose yam was biggest, whose produce looked the best, what items should have been kept at home, along with the latest happenings in the district.

Those were simple days of uncomplicated pleasures and the warm fellowship of ordinary people rejoicing and giving thanks for ordinary gifts from an extraordinary God. Sometimes we look back and things seem much better than they might actually have been. There were the great Harvests when the weather was good and farms prospered. But there were also the lean years, when drought and other factors brought hardships and the Harvest looked a little malnourished.

Traditions are important to the human experience. They establish milestones and provide memories that connect us to each other and to the past. It is my Prayer that the tradition of Harvest will be an entrenched feature of Christian life and that each generation will add their own special flavor to it. Let us all participate in Harvest and let us give the best that we can give, small or great, and in so doing, give honour to God and encouragement to each other.

"Therefore, brethren, stand fast, and hold the traditions which ye have been taught, whether by word, or our epistle."
- 2 Thessalonians 2:15 (KJV)

GIVING FROM 'BORROWED GOODS.'

The quotation; "it is better to give than to receive" is a very familiar one. Often it is used as the ultimate form of persuading someone to give away something that they would prefer to keep. Many times the person quoting is more interested in the receiving, than in promoting the use of Scripture, or Biblical behavior. I believe that the ability to give generously is a blessing, but that the desire to give selflessly, is a gift.

Giving is something we all do to some degree, but for many of us, we do not suffer from an abundance of generosity. We may enjoy giving to those we love . . . our spouse, our children, our parents, our relatives and our friends. We enjoy their expressions of appreciation, and feel good that our act of giving has made them feel good. We also give, when we see a need or situation that moves us, we feel compelled to help and to make a difference in the life of a needy person. We enjoy the sense of satisfaction that comes from knowing that we had the capacity to care, and the ability to express that care in a tangible way.

Giving is something we all do, but our motivations and expectations vary widely. Sometimes we give for less noble reasons. Sometimes to get rid of someone who has been pestering us, to make a good impression, or to get rid of things we do not want. Most if not all of us can identify with giving for the wrong reasons, but we can also identify times when we gave without thought to how it looked, how we would benefit, or what was in it for us.

As Christians, we are called to 'higher order' giving. Giving that is less about ourselves and more about others. Giving that is more about giving pleasure to God than experiencing self-satisfaction. This kind of giving generally results in our ending up with a 'good feeling' and an enhanced sense of well-being. But these are not the reasons why we give, they are the value-added benefits of our Christian generosity.

The Bible has a lot to say about giving, and about how we relate to our possessions. It regards possessions as gifts we receive from a loving and generous God. As a matter of fact, it regards these gifts not as things we own, but as things that have been loaned to us, we are really tenants on the earth. One day we will have to leave our earthly residence, and we won't be able to take the furniture or appliances with us when we leave, not even the clothes on our backs can be taken with us.

How we relate to the things we have, are a telling indicator of what is important to us, but more importantly, who is important to us. That is why the Bible tells us that where our treasure is, there is our heart also.

If we have a right relationship with God, we will have a right relationship with our possessions (the gifts he has loaned to us). When we have this relationship with Him, we are able to give to others and to God, in the manner He is giving to us which is always generously and cheerfully. How is your giving?

"But this I say: he who sows sparingly will also reap sparingly, and

he who sows bountifully will also reap bountifully. So let each one give as he purposes in his heart, not grudgingly or of necessity; for God loves a cheerful giver. And God is able to make all grace abound toward you, that you, always having all sufficiency in all things, may have abundance for every good work. As it is written: He has dispersed abroad, He has given to the poor; His righteousness endures forever. Now may He who gives seed to the sower, and bread for food, supply and multiply the seed you have sown and increase the fruits of your righteousness." - 2 Corinthians 9: 6-10 (NKJV)

THE RHYTHM OF THE SEASONS OF LIFE

For those of us who live in societies with a tropical climate, not much attention is paid to the seasons. In fact, there are no dramatic changes between one season and the next, and our daily activities are not greatly influenced by weather, except perhaps the rainy season which we refer to as "weather".

But in some societies, life is governed largely by the seasons. Each season comes with its distinctive feature, with the greatest contrast being between, winter and summer. In those places, harsh winters with freezing cold weather and abundant snow and ice, force people to live their lives indoors and to venture outside only when covered by layers of warm clothing. They ignore the unique environmental characteristics of the seasons at their peril. They have learned to adapt to the changes that each season brings and for them the adjustments they have to make come naturally, if not always easily.

Farmers know what it is to adapt to the seasons. The experienced farmer knows when it is 'planting season' and when it is ' reaping season.' During reaping season, he conserves and organizes his affairs so that when the planting season comes around and there is no produce to reap, he and his family will still be able to live.

But there is also such a thing as the 'season of our lives". We experience our summers and our winters, our autumns and our springs, our planting season and our reaping season, our pruning season and our 'resting' season. There is a rhythm to life. An ebb and flow to our existence. We experience periods of indescribable joy and moments of unbearable pain. We have periods of boundless energy and times of unexplained lethargy. We have periods of exceptional successes and seasons of seemingly endless failures.

None of us however, has 'one season lives'. In our frozen "winters" we may feel that "spring" will never come, but it will. In our joyous "summers" of cloudless skies, we may feel that the season of dark clouds will not intrude, but it will. Each of us is given a special capacity to handle the seasons of our lives, some of us are better at it than others.

But if we are to make the most of the gift of life that God gives us, we have to learn to work in harmony with the seasons and not discordantly against them. To adapt skillfully to the changes that are beyond our control. To learn the secret of the lily that lay buried underground as an unattractive and unassuming bulb, knowing that one day, when the season changes, it will burst out from the ground and dazzle the world with the beauty of its bloom.

'To everything there is a season, and a time to every purpose under the heaven: A time to be born and a time to die; a time plant and a time to pluck up that which is planted; a time to kill, and a time to heal; a time to break down and a time to build up; a time to weep and a time to laugh, a time to mourn and a time to dance......... I have seen the travail which God hath given to the sons of men to be exercised in it. He hath made everything beautiful in his time: - Ecclesiastes 3:1-11 (excerpts KJV)

SCRIPTURE HAS A POWER THAT'S UNDENIABLE

The Books of the Bible
Time tested and reliable
Scripture has a power that's undeniable

Genesis, Exodus, Leviticus, Numbers and Deuteronomy
Joshua, Judges, Ruth, 1st & 2nd Peter, 1st & 2nd Kings,
1st & 2nd Chronicles, Ezra, Nehemiah, Esther, Job and Psalms
Proverbs, Ecclesiastes, Song of Solomon, Isaiah, Jeremiah,
Lamentation
Ezekiel, Daniel, Hosea, Joel, Amos Obadiah, Jonah, Micah Nahum,
Habakkuk and Zephaniah, Haggai, Zechariah, Malachi

The Books of the Bible
Their wisdoms verifiable
Scripture has a power that's undeniable

Matthew, Mark, Luke And John Acts and Romans
1st Corinthian, 2nd Corinthian Galatians, Ephesian, Philippians
Colossians, Thessalonian, 1 and 2 1st Timothy 2nd Timothy Titus,
Philemon
Hebrews, James, 1& 2 Peter 1&2 John 3 John Judea and Revelation

The Books of the Bible
Their wisdoms verifiable
Scripture has a power that's undeniable

"How blessed is the man who finds wisdom and the man who gains understanding? For her profit is better than the profit of silver and her gain better than fine gold. She is more precious than jewels; And nothing you desire compares with her". - Proverbs 3:13-15

GEMS OF TRUTH

HIDDEN TREASURE, HOLY POWER

EXTRAVAGANT WORSHIP

GEMS OF TRUTH

Reading is one of the greatest abilities that a person can acquire. It is the gateway to knowledge, the passport to places that we may never reach physically, a window into the lives and lifestyles of diverse peoples, a vehicle that transports us to thoughts and ideas that inspire and elevate us. It opens the door of understanding to many of life's complexities, and it is companionship and community to the alone and isolated.

For us as Christians, Reading is a lifeline to the divine. God has graciously provided us with his written word and made it available to those who will make the effort to read it. I have found reading the Bible an essential activity in my life. The Bible has become a real companion. Its words correct me when I am in the wrong, encourage me when I am low, inspire me to do more and become better, remind me of the greatness and goodness of God, and assure me, that right will ultimately conquer wrong. That in the end, God rules and His will, will be done.

The rigorous debates of Paul stimulate my thinking. The raw pragmatism of James challenges me to be grounded. The excitement and drama of the Acts, challenges me to expect more from God. The Gospels in their colorful narrative, brings the life and message of Jesus to life. The Letters to the churches weave a rich tapestry of heroic acts, amidst disappointing failures, all mixed with evidence of God's unending work of redemption and restoration.

The Old Testament with its heroes and villains, saints and sinners, powerful warriors and weak rulers, faithful and unfaithful children of God, childlike images, and adults' only stories, is not easily digested. Its turbulence and violence sometimes assaults the senses. But it powerfully portrays the sovereign God at work, in a world seemingly consumed with provoking him to wrath. It is also filled with moments of divine awe, stories of selfless love and devotion, and expressions of praise and worship, that lift us into heavenly places.

For me, the Old Testament is filled with precious gems of truth. Hidden in stories of judgement, punishment and pain, are words of peculiar beauty and inspiration. The Bible may contain what some would consider to be "boring" parts. But it is, from beginning to end, a thoroughly rich and exciting book. If we treat the Bible as if we are eating a 'box lunch', if we just 'cut and swallow,' we may not truly enjoy it, or worse, we may even experience indigestion.

We need to treat the reading of the Bile as an amazing dining experience. An exquisite meal, prepared by a Master Chef, served on the finest china, in a room tastefully designed to our personal liking, and in the company of our favorite people. In this setting, we can feast on the word, savour its delicate flavors and delight in the moment. At the end of such a meal, the Master Chef will smile down on us and say to himself, this meal was worth preparing, because all who dined were glad that they did.

I commend to you this beautiful passage in Isaiah that gives a glimpse of our Lord, graciously waiting to enjoy our company. *"Therefore, the Lord waits to be gracious to you, and therefore he exalts himself to show mercy to you."* - Isaiah 30:18 (NIV)

HIDDEN TREASURE, HOLY POWER

The Book of Acts is filled with stories of God's involvement in the life of his people and the demonstration of his power and love in the challenges of their lives. In some situations, his presence and power are manifested in dramatic and powerful ways. In others, his presence is muted and almost unnoticeable. But in all situations, His presence makes the difference.

The characters in the stories found in the Book of Acts, are for the most part ordinary people. Persons who if they were living today, we would walk past them in the street and not take notice. But they were people who were being used by God to establish his church, spread his gospel, and change the world.

They must have had the everyday concerns and issues that regular people had to contend with then, just as regular people have today. . . how to provide for their families, what to cook, who to marry, where to live, how to prepare for the future, how to bring up children, how to resolve differences, who to worship etc. In the midst of the powerful manifestations of the Holy Spirit, and the remarkable evidence of God at work in their lives, there were still the basic issues of life and of living.

We are filled with wonder at their experiences and the things that happened to them and around them, but we do not leave with a sense that these were supermen or superwomen, we slowly realize that the 'super' in their lives was the presence and power of God. Doubtful Thomas, timid Timothy, rough and ready Peter, no-nonsense James and the others, would have lived their anonymous lives and been laid to rest like any other ordinary persons of their time. But since they met Jesus their lives were changed and so too was their work, worth and impact. Their stories are being repeated in every generation, as God reaches ordinary and not so ordinary people and pours into them his extraordinary grace and power.

If you are wondering about your ability to be used by God, or whether or not you can make a difference in His Kingdom, I encourage you to offer yourself to Him and allow Him to mold you and shape you into the perfect instrument he has designed you to be, you will be amazed at the result. Paul understood this and in the following passage, gives us essential words of encouragement that should strengthen and guide us, as God pours into our unique jars of clay, his exquisite treasures.

"But we have this treasure in jars of clay, to show that the surpassing power belongs to God and not to us. We are afflicted in every way but not crushed, perplexed, but not driven to despair, persecuted but not forsaken, struck down, but not destroyed; always carrying in the body the death of Jesus, so that the life of Jesus may be manifested in our bodies . . . So, we do not lose heart. Though our outer self is wasting away our inner self is being renewed day by day. For this momentary affliction is preparing for us an eternal weight of glory beyond all comparison, as we look not to the things that are seen but to the things that are unseen. For the things that are seen are transient, but the things that are unseen are eternal." - 2 Cor. 4:7-18 (ESV)

EXTRAVAGANT WORSHIP

Let us pull out from the treasure trove of amazing Bible Stories and lessons, the story of Mary Magdalene, and what some would describe as her extravagant act of worship. Her act, unlike the other story of worship regarding the poor widow and her "mite" of offering to the Lord, was not quiet, discreet or unobtrusive.

Jesus was a guest in Simon's home and as usual, was surrounded by a crowd of people anxious to hear him speak and to see him perform miracles. Into this crowded room burst Mary. Her love for Jesus blinding her to the crowd, deafening her to their comments, driving her to express her love in her own unique and feminine way.

It is generally believed that this is the same Mary who had been rescued from a scandalous past, from personal failure and emptiness and given a new life. A life that had new meaning, new purpose, new purity and a righteousness that she never dreamed possible. Jesus had changed her life. She knew her past. She knew her pain and she knew the enormous debt of gratitude that she owed to Jesus.

Her offering was costly by any standard. It was something that meant much to her. It was a precious perfume, securely stored in a bottle made of alabaster. The container itself was valuable. She might have had it for a long time, jealously guarding it, and waiting for the perfect occasion when she would release its fragrant contents. It would have to be that "once in a life time occasion", because once poured out, that would it. There could be no "second' use.

But this "special occasion" was not about her. It was not about anointing herself, for her own purposes with this precious perfume. It was not about drawing attention to herself, or about gaining the admiration of others for her sophisticated taste, and fragrant allure. It was all about worship, extravagant worship perhaps, but to Mary nothing was too good, or too valuable, or too much to express her love and deep regard.

But this "extravagant" act of worship opened a floodgate of criticism from the onlookers. How vain to even have spent so much money on perfume? How carnal to think that the holy Son of God, the great teacher, would appreciate a gift so worldly and frivolous? How familiar and presumptuous to even attempt to touch him, much less anoint him? But this was who she was, this was what she had, this was what she could do, and this was the best worship she could offer.

The crowd and the critics were put in their place by Jesus. Their sudden interest in the poor and in assisting them was dismissed by Jesus for the hypocrisy, insincerity and blatant farce that it was. He knew that this was a special act of preparation for his imminent death. He knew that their presence and professed interest and support for him would evaporate like the perfume. That many of them would leave him, some to join the crowds that would be shouting, Crucify Him! Crucify Him!

Let us, unreservedly, give to our Lord, our unique and extravagant worship.

TIME, TIMING, GOD's DIRECTION and AUTHORITY

Genesis 8: 22 *While the earth remains, Seedtime and harvest, And cold and heat, And summer and winter, And day and night Shall not cease."*

Job 14:5 *Since his days are determined, The number of his months is with You; And his limits You have set so that he cannot pass.*

Romans 8:28 *And we know that God causes all things to work together for good to those who love God, to those who are called according to His purpose.*

Daniel 2:21 *It is He who changes the times and the epochs; He removes kings and establishes kings; He gives wisdom to wise men And knowledge to men of understanding*

2 Corinthians 6:2 *- For he saith, I have heard thee in a time accepted, and in the day of salvation have I succoured thee: behold, now is the accepted time; behold, now is the day of salvation*

Mark 13:32 *- But of that day and that hour knoweth no man, no, not the angels which are in heaven, neither the Son, but the Father.*

James 4:14 *- Whereas ye know not what shall be on the morrow. For what is your life? It is even a vapour, that appeareth for a little time, and then vanisheth away.*

Psalms 90:2 *- Before the mountains were brought forth, or ever thou hadst formed the earth and the world, even from everlasting to everlasting, thou art God.*

Psalms 90:4 *- For a thousand years in thy sight are but as yesterday when it is past, and as a watch in the night.*

Psalm 39:5-6 *Behold, You have made my days as handbreadths, And my lifetime as nothing in Your sight; Surely every man at his best is a mere breath. Selah. "Surely every man walks about as a phantom; Surely they make an uproar for nothing; He amasses riches and does not know who will gather them*

"To every [thing there is] a season, and a time to every purpose under the heaven: A time to be born, and a time to die; a time to plant, and a time to pluck up that which is] planted; A time to kill, and a time to heal; a time to break down, and a time to build up; A time to weep, and a time to laugh; a time to mourn, and a time to dance; A time to cast away stones, and a time to gather stones together; a time to embrace, and a time to refrain from embracing; A time to get, and a time to lose; a time to keep, and a time to cast away; A time to rend, and a time to sew; a time to keep silence, and a time to speak; A time to love, and a time to hate; a time of war, and a time of peace" - Ecclesiastes 3:1-8

THE VALUE OF TIME WITH GOD IN IT

GOD's TIME IS ALL THE TIME

THE VALUE OF TIME WITH GOD IN IT

For many of us, time seems to be just racing by. Some persons have even expressed the view that days were now shorter and not the twenty-four (24) hours that they are supposed to be. The truth is that days are still twenty-four (24) hours long, hours are still sixty (60) minutes long and it still takes sixty (60) seconds to make a minute.

However, we end up at the end of the day feeling that there are not enough hours in the day to accomplish all that we want to do. Sometimes it is because we have so much to do that we are unable to catch up, but sometimes it could be because we are on low energy, or have things to do that do not excite us, or things that we do not enjoy, or things we may even dislike.

So after six months into a year, we may find that a number of things that we had on our list of priorities have not been touched, are at the bottom of the pile, or are in danger of falling off the list all together. We may have given up on resolutions and so do not call them by that name, but they are still resolutions, a rose by any other name is still a rose.

Resolutions, goals, plans expectations or whatever we may call them, are helpful tools in making the most of our time. Without them we could end up living without a sense of direction or journeying through life aimlessly. We may not have written them down or identified them very clearly to ourselves, but I believe each of us have a set of things we want to accomplish by a certain time.

But what if we are falling behind, what if we feel that at the "markers" we set towards achieving our goals are not in alignment with what we had planned? Do we forget about our plans and just "go with the flow"? Or do we use the "markers" as milestones, to take stock, reassess our goals and resolutions and then make the necessary adjustments? As we do our reassessment and adjustments we must be reminded that "except the Lord build the house, they labor in vain that build it." He needs to be central to all that we do or attempt to do.

"Commit thy works unto the LORD, and thy thoughts shall be established". - Proverbs 16:3

"So teach us to number our days, that we may apply our hearts unto wisdom".- Psalms 90:12 -

"Trust in the Lord with all your heart and lean not on your own understanding; in all your ways acknowledge him, and he will make your paths straight. Do not be wise in your own eyes; fear the Lord and shun evil. This will bring health to your body and nourishment to your bones. Honor the Lord with your wealth and with the first fruits of all your crops; then your barns will be filled to overflowing and your vats will brim over with new wine." - Proverbs 3:5-9 (NIV)

GOD'S TIME IS ALL THE TIME

The idea of traveling back and forward in time has fascinated mankind for centuries. Inventors have tried to create 'time machines.' Historians have tried to recapture the past from stories and artifacts that illustrate how life was. Writers have stretched their imaginations to create stories that depict how they imagine life will be in the future. Mankind has not been able however to travel back in time, or journey into the future literally. We live in the present.

Last year like all the years before that, is history. We carry its memories, but we cannot relive the good ones or undo the bad ones. Each new year and each and every new day, down to each new moment, is God's gift to each of us. A new page, a clean canvas, on which, with His help, we can create a masterpiece, by his Power, for His glory.

I pray that God will become even more real to you each day, throughout the years and that He will walk closely with you as you step into the uncharted paths that are in front of you.

"Brethren, I count not myself to have apprehended: but this one thing I do, forgetting those things which are behind, and reaching forth unto those things which are before, I press toward the mark for the prize of the high calling of God in Christ Jesus". - Philippians 3:13-14

But, beloved, be not ignorant of this one thing, that one day [is] with the Lord as a thousand years, and a thousand years as one day - 2 Peter 3:8 -

My times [are] in thy hand: deliver me from the hand of mine enemies, and from them that persecute me - Psalms 31:15

"That in the dispensation of the fullness of times he might gather together in one all things in Christ, both which are in heaven, and which are on earth; even in him." - Ephesians 1:10

―――――――――――――

HIS GRACE IS SUFFICIENT

John 1:14 *And the Word became flesh and dwelt among us, and we have seen his glory, glory as of the only Son from the Father, full of grace and truth*

John 1:15-17 *(John bore witness about him, and cried out, "This was he of whom I said, 'He who comes after me ranks before me, because he was before me.'") And from his fullness we have all received, grace upon grace. For the law was given through Moses; grace and truth came through Jesus Christ*

Acts 4:33 *And with great power the apostles were giving their testimony to the resurrection of the Lord Jesus, and great grace was upon them all*

2 Corinthians 12:8-9 *Three times I pleaded with the Lord about this, that it should leave me. But he said to me, "My grace is sufficient for you, for my power is made perfect in weakness." Therefore I will boast all the more gladly of my weaknesses, so that the power of Christ may rest upon me*

Hebrews 4:16 *Let us then with confidence draw near to the throne of grace, that we may receive mercy and find grace to help in time of need*

Acts 20:32 *And now I commend you to God and to the word of his grace, which is able to build you up and to give you the inheritance among all those who are sanctified.*

Hebrews 12:15 *See to it that no one fails to obtain the grace of God; that no "root of bitterness" springs up and causes trouble, and by it many become defiled*

1 Peter 5:10 *And after you have suffered a little while, the God of all grace, who has called you to his eternal glory in Christ, will himself restore, confirm, strengthen, and establish you*

Romans 5:1-2 *Therefore, since we have been justified by faith, we have peace with God through our Lord Jesus Christ. Through him we have also obtained access by faith into this grace in which we stand, and we rejoice in hope of the glory of God.*

"But God, being rich in mercy, because of the great love with which he loved us, even when we were dead in our trespasses, made us alive together with Christ— by grace you have been saved—and raised us up with him and seated us with him in the heavenly places in Christ Jesus, so that in the coming ages he might show the immeasurable riches of his grace in kindness toward us in Christ Jesus. For by grace you have been saved through faith. And this is not your own doing; it is the gift of God, not a result of works, so that no one may boast" - Ephesians 2:4-9

GRACE AND PEACE FROM OUR RISEN LORD

GRACE AND PEACE

GRACE AND PEACE IN ABUNDANCE

GRACE AND PEACE FROM OUR RISEN LORD

As Christians, we declare with joy, that Jesus Christ is alive. He conquered the powerful Jewish leaders. He conquered Pilate and his Roman forces. He conquered the cross and its shame. He conquered death and its strangle-hold on humanity. He conquered sin and its chains. He lives, and He reigns as Lord.

This declaration has over the centuries been welcomed by millions of people from all walks of life. People from diverse races, cultures, ages, gender, status and places, have found this declaration a message of hope and transformation. It has also been met with doubt, disbelief and even ridicule. There are those who cannot embrace the possibility of a God who would allow himself to be killed, and then to defy the laws of nature and come back to life, three days later.

Very few people deny that Jesus Christ really lived on earth. Most agree that he was a good man and a great teacher. He is an undeniably important figure in history. The largest religion in the world bears his name. The Bible which carries his message, is the most popular book in history. Even the Calendar pays tribute to him (BC & AD). But many have a difficulty with the Divine or supernatural aspects of his life.

His virgin birth, the miracles he did, the claims he makes to being the Son of God and the claims of his resurrection, are hard for many to accept. Some struggle with serious intellectual doubt, and others use questions of his divinity, as smokescreens to avoid the compelling claims he makes for their affection and obedience. His resurrection is for them, an inconvenient truth.

Reflections on the Salutations of the Apostle Paul, reminds us that the story of Jesus was as controversial then, in his time, as it is now, in our time. The truth of his Resurrection was a 'hot topic' and was central to the preaching of the Apostles and the beliefs of the early church.

In his Greetings to the Galatians, Paul dives right into the issue and states his position clearly and forcefully. He introduced himself as an Apostle sent by Jesus Christ, who God raised from the dead. At the time of writing this Letter, it would have been foolish of Paul to have made such a bold assertion if he were not personally convinced of it, and certain that his assertion would stand up to scrutiny.

Paul's Salutations in the Epistle to the Galatians is a message that should reinforce our faith, as we seek to be true servants of the Risen Lord. *"Paul, an Apostle, sent not from men, nor by man, but by Jesus Christ and God the Father, who raised him from the dead, and all the brethren with me. To the churches in Galatia: Grace and peace from God our Father and the Lord Jesus Christ, who gave himself for our sins to rescue us from the present evil age, according to the will of our God and Father. To whom be glory for ever and ever Amen".* - Galatians 1: 1-5 (NIV)

GRACE AND PEACE

Paul's Salutations or Greetings to the Corinthians, is similar in tone and content to his Salutation in the Book of Romans. This Letter must have been a difficult one for Paul to write, because he had to confront issues no Christian Leader wants to deal with, among the people that they lead.

The Church in Corinth had problems, huge problems. It was a spirited church that 'flowed' in the spiritual gifts but was stagnant with the spiritual graces. It was a divided and contentious congregation that had succeeded in making even the solemn observance of the Lord's Supper a disgraceful display of gluttony and selfishness. Sexual immorality was rampant and some acts that were condoned by some in the church were outrageous, even by the very corrupt standards of Corinthian society.

Factions had been formed in the church around misplaced loyalties to their Founders and Leaders. There were those who seemed to have held Paul and the work he had done in establishing the church in contempt. In the Letter, Paul had to defend his authority and Apostleship as a result of the undermining that had taken place.

Even though Paul was writing this Letter after getting all the bad news of the goings on in Corinth however, he writes with a shepherd's heart, and his Salutation is again remarkably gracious. Even though the church had such severe disciplinary issues, and the behavior of some of its members had brought disgrace to the name of Christ, the church itself stood as a witness to the redemptive power of Christ, and within its numbers, were those who were faithful in their walk.

Paul greets the church and speaks to those who were sanctified, called to be saints, those who called on the name of the Lord. Paul seems to write with an underlying expectation that the truth of the Gospel and the renewing power of Christ could and would create change in this wayward church.

He probably understood more than most, the serious external challenges faced by the Christians in Corinth. It was one of the most immoral cities in its day and pagan religious influences dominated the culture. His salutation offers them grace and peace and reaffirms the unique nature of their calling and the keeping power of the one who had called them.

"Grace and peace to you from our Lord Jesus Christ. I always give thanks for you because of his grace given you in Christ Jesus. For in him you have been enriched in every way - in all your speaking and in all your knowledge - because our testimony about Christ was confirmed in you. Therefore, you do not lack any spiritual gift as you eagerly await for our Lord Jesus Christ to be revealed. He will keep you strong to the end, so that you will be blameless on the day of our Lord Jesus Christ. God, who has called you into Fellowship with his son Jesus Christ our Lord, is faithful." - 1 Corinthians 1:3- 9(NIV)

GRACE AND PEACE IN ABUNDANCE

The Book of First Peter is one of the shorter books in the Bible. In its five Chapters however, the Apostle covers a lot of ground, instructing and inspiring his readers to living Christ-centred, God-honouring and exemplary lives as followers of Jesus Christ.

The Apostle Peter is one of the most colorful characters in the New Testament. Jesus saw something in him and called him to be among the first set of Disciples. He was faithful but flawed. He was a defender but also a denier. He was courageous, but sometimes a coward. He was targeted by Satan to be sifted as wheat, but Jesus prayed for him and he went on to become one of the most influential Preachers of all time.

The book of First Peter is powerful not only in its Message, but in who God chose to be the Messenger. Peter was not the educated, religiously driven and international Citizen that Paul was, nor the authoritative Church Leader that James was, or even the beloved teacher and mystic that John became. He simply introduced himself as Peter, an Apostle of Jesus Christ. He was a Messenger.

He was writing to Christians, strangers in the world, scattered throughout Pontus, Galatia, Cappadocia and Bithynia. These Christians, a mixture of converted Jews and Gentiles were experiencing great challenges and suffering, because of their faith and commitment to Jesus Christ and this new religion called Christianity.

Peter must have been painfully aware of the suffering that they had been facing and immense challenges these presented to their faith and trust in God. Many must have been questioning the value of this new faith and asking why it came with so much testing and trials. Questions that in this enlightened twenty first century, more than two thousand years later, continue to be asked by Christians all over the world.

Peter does not provide 'pat' answers. Neither does he dodge the difficult issues. His approach is more prescriptive than reactive. He not only acknowledges the reality of suffering, but emphasizes that it is to be expected and presents Christ, the "suffering Saviour", as the reference point for the Believer.

He greets them by saying: "Grace and Peace be yours in abundance." This is a greeting he shares with the Apostle Paul. A prayer that they experience God's Grace. His undeserved favour, redemption and blessing and His Peace, His Shalom. His peace that passes understanding. A peace described in the NIV study notes as: 'the total well-being and security that only God can provide, and that He does provide fully only to those who are at peace with Him".

I encourage you to read, meditate on and immerse yourself in the Book of First Peter and discover the rich provisions of Grace and peace embedded in God's Word.

"Though you have not seen Him, you love Him, and even though you do not see Him now, you believe in Him, and are filled with an inexpressible and glorious joy. For you are receiving the goal of your faith, the salvation of your souls." - 1 Peter 1:8-9 (NIV)

EXALTED AS HEAD OVER ALL

Psalm 145:1-7 *I will exalt you, my God the King; I will praise your name for ever and ever. Every day I will praise you and extol your name for ever and ever. Great is the Lord and most worthy of praise; his greatness no one can fathom. One generation commends your works to another; they tell of your mighty acts. They speak of the glorious splendor of your majesty—and I will meditate on your wonderful works. They tell of the power of your awesome works—and I will proclaim your great deeds. They will celebrate your abundant goodness and joyfully sing of your righteousness.*

Psalm 95

O come, let us sing unto the LORD: let us make a joyful noise to the rock of our salvation. Let us come before his presence with thanksgiving, and make a joyful noise unto him with psalms. For the LORD is a great God, and a great King above all gods. In his hand are the deep places of the earth: the strength of the hills is his also. The sea is his, and he made it: and his hands formed the dry land. O come, let us worship and bow down: let us kneel before the LORD our maker.

Psalm 100 *Make a joyful noise unto the LORD, all ye lands. Serve the LORD with gladness: come before his presence with singing. Know ye that the LORD he is God: it is he that hath made us, and not we ourselves; we are his people, and the sheep of his pasture. Enter into his gates with thanksgiving, and into his courts with praise: be thankful unto him, and bless his name. For the LORD is good; his mercy is everlasting; and his truth endureth to all generations*

1 Chronicles 16:28-30,34 *O nations of the world, recognize the Lord, recognize that the Lord is glorious and strong. Give to the Lord the glory he deserves! Bring your offering and come into his presence. Worship the Lord in all his holy splendor. Let all the earth tremble before him. The world stands firm and cannot be shaken. Give thanks to the Lord, for he is good! His faithful love endures forever*

'Yours, O LORD, is the greatness and the power and the glory and the majesty and the splendor, for everything in heaven and earth is yours. Yours, O LORD, is the kingdom; you are exalted as head over all" -1 Chronicles 29:11-13

OUR GOD REIGNS

OUR GOD OF SALVATION

STAND UP

OUR GOD REIGNS

The writings of the Prophet Isaiah are rich in imagery and he takes us on a journey that is filled with action and movement. In one breath, we are asked to weep and mourn and in the other, we are commanded to shout for joy and to celebrate in dance.

It is a Book of deep emotions. A Book that expresses the range and richness of God's responses to man's condition . . . from his anger and Judgement to his gentle affection and redeeming love. It has some of the most quoted portions of the Bible. It affirms in strong, graphic and touching words, God's great love for us. A sentiment repeated throughout the book and conveyed in a variety of ways.

In Chapter 52, Isaiah reminds us of an old and eternal truth "our God reigns". It is a short statement but powerful in its impact. It is a word of encouragement to the discouraged. A word of hope to the insecure. A word of courage to the fearful. A word of strength to the weak. A word of peace to the anxious. A word of redemption to the falling. A word of warning to the careless. A word of healing to the wounded and a word of life to the dying. We can go through life with confidence and courage, knowing that 'Our God Reigns.'

Awake, awake, Clothe yourself in your strength, O Zion; Clothe yourself in your beautiful garments, O Jerusalem, the holy city; For the uncircumcised and the unclean Will no longer come into you. Shake yourself from the dust, rise up, O captive Jerusalem; Loose yourself from the chains around your neck, O captive daughter of Zion.

For thus says the LORD, "You were sold for nothing and you will be redeemed without money." For thus says the Lord GOD, "My people went down at the first into Egypt to reside there; then the Assyrian oppressed them without cause. "Now therefore, what do I have here," declares the LORD, "seeing that My people have been taken away without cause?" Again the LORD declares, "Those who rule over them howl, and My name is continually blasphemed all day long. "Therefore My people shall know My name; therefore in that day I am the one who is speaking, 'Here I am.'"

How lovely on the mountains are the feet of him who brings good news, Who announces peace And brings good news of happiness, Who announces salvation, And says to Zion, "Your God reigns!" Listen! Your watchmen lift up their voices, They shout joyfully together; For they will see with their own eyes When the LORD restores Zion. Break forth, shout joyfully together, You waste places of Jerusalem; For the LORD has comforted His people, He has redeemed Jerusalem. The LORD has bared His holy arm in the sight of all the nations, That all the ends of the earth may see The salvation of our God.

Depart, depart, go out from there, Touch nothing unclean; Go out of the midst of her, purify yourselves, You who carry the vessels of the LORD. But you will not go out in haste, Nor will you go as fugitives; For the LORD will go before you, And the God of Israel will be your rear guard.

Behold, My servant will prosper, He will be high and lifted up and greatly exalted. Just as many were astonished at you, My people, So His appearance was marred more than any man, And His form more than the sons of men. Thus He will sprinkle many nations, Kings will shut their mouths on account of Him; For what had not been told them they will see, And what they had not heard they will understand - Isaiah 52 (New American Standard Bible)

OUR GOD OF SALVATION

Isaiah's writings provide us with great insight into God's relationship with his people. He presents a picture of God as a God of Judgement. A God who will execute severe judgement when his people reject his way and are unrepentant about their wrong doings. But he also paints a picture of God as a God of Salvation. God desires to save His people, and will take extreme measures and make great sacrifices, to bring them salvation.

We are introduced by Isaiah to the suffering Saviour, the lamb that would be slain for our redemption. Isaiah acknowledges that: "we all like sheep have gone astray, each of us have turned to his own way;" We are therefore all deserving of God's Judgement. The suffering Saviour steps in however, and sacrificially offers himself as our substitute. Taking unto himself the guilt, the pain and the price of our waywardness.

Let us take time to reflect on our Lord Jesus Christ, who paid the price for our waywardness with his own life. Let us recommit ourselves to living as redeemed people. Fully committed to demonstrating in our lives, His resurrection power and his sacrificial love.

"Who hath believed our report? and to whom is the arm of the LORD revealed?

For he shall grow up before him as a tender plant, and as a root out of a dry ground: he hath no form nor comeliness; and when we shall see him, there is no beauty that we should desire Him. He is despised and rejected of men; a man of sorrows, and acquainted with grief: and we hid as it were our faces from him; he was despised, and we esteemed him not.

Surely he hath borne our griefs, and carried our sorrows: yet we did esteem him stricken, smitten of God, and afflicted. But he was wounded for our transgressions, he was bruised for our iniquities: the chastisement of our peace was upon him; and with his stripes we are healed.

All we like sheep have gone astray; we have turned everyone to his own way; and the LORD hath laid on him the iniquity of us all.

He was oppressed, and he was afflicted, yet he opened not his mouth: he is brought as a lamb to the slaughter, and as a sheep before her shearers is dumb, so he openeth not his mouth. He was taken from prison and from judgment: and who shall declare his generation? for he was cut off out of the land of the living: for the transgression of my people was he stricken.

And he made his grave with the wicked, and with the rich in his death; because he had done no violence, neither was any deceit in his mouth. Yet it pleased the LORD to bruise him; he hath put him to grief: when thou shalt make his soul an offering for sin, he shall see his seed, he shall prolong his days, and the pleasure of the LORD shall prosper in his hand.

He shall see of the travail of his soul, and shall be satisfied: by his knowledge shall my righteous servant justify many; for he shall bear their iniquities. Therefore will I divide him a portion with the great, and he shall divide the spoil with the strong; because he hath poured out his soul unto death: and he was numbered with the transgressors; and he bare the sin of many, and made intercession for the transgressors". - Isaiah 53 KJV

STAND UP

The Church is not going to win the approval of everyone. There are times when the church must stand alone. Jesus himself demonstrated this in his life, and in the nature of his death. It is his approval that matters.

Each of us is called to express our Faith in the place in which we live. For some, it is some quiet simple place, where the values of our community and the values of our faith are very similar. In those places, to be a good Christian, is to be a good Citizen.

But some of us live out our Faith in far more complicated settings and the values of those around us are far from Christian and in some cases, are even opposed to them. In those complex settings, the thoughtful Christian struggles with working out an appropriate response and how to navigate this terrain in a way that ultimately advances the mission of Christ.

In this complex mix, emerges a diversity of responses that reflect the diversity of the church. We have the activists and politically savvy; the Diplomat and networker; the strategist and schemer; the philosopher and thought leader; the street operator and demonstrator; the foot soldier and the Field-marshall. All have their time and their place. Each of us must seek to find our place and play our unique role, but none of us can afford to watch from the sidelines.

Today we as Christians are called to stand. We must stand as brothers and sisters, and together declare that we will not be silent about the things that are offensive to our God. Let us stand up and speak, as uncomfortable as it may be for some, so that generations to come, will continue to enjoy this freedom that today we so easily take for granted, to stand up for their faith in Jesus Christ. Stand up! Stand up for Jesus!

"Why do the heathens rage and the peoples plot in vain? The kings of the earth take their stand and the rulers gather together against the Lord and against His Anointed One. .... Now, Lord, consider their threats and enable your servants to speak your words with great boldness. Stretch out your hand to heal and perform miraculous signs and wonders through the name of your holy servant Jesus. After they prayed, the place where they were meeting was shaken, and they were all filled with the Holy Spirit and spoke the word of God boldly." - Acts 4:25-31 (NIV)

WE GIVE YOU THANKS, O LORD GOD ALMIGHTY

Psalm 100 - Make a joyful noise unto the LORD, all ye lands; Serve the LORD with gladness: come before his presence with singing; Know ye that the LORD he is God: it is he that hath made us, and not we ourselves; we are his people, and the sheep of his pasture; Enter into his gates with thanksgiving, and into his courts with praise: be thankful unto him, and bless his name;For the LORD is good; his mercy is everlasting; and his truth endureth to all generations.

2 Chronicles 5:13 The trumpeters and musicians joined in unison to give praise and thanks to the LORD. Accompanied by trumpets, cymbals and other instruments, the singers raised their voices in praise to the LORD and sang: "He is good; his love endures forever." Then the temple of the LORD was filled with the cloud,

Rev 11:17.. saying: " We give You thanks, O Lord God Almighty, The One who is and who was and who is to come, Because You have taken Your great power and reigned

"O give thanks to the LORD, for He is good; for His loving kindness is everlasting. Then say, "Save us, O God of our salvation, and gather us and deliver us from the nations, to give thanks to Your holy name, and glory in Your praise." Blessed be the LORD, the God of Israel, from everlasting even to everlasting. Then all the people said, "Amen," and praised the LORD" - 1 Chron 16:34-36

GOD IS ALWAYS GOOD

GIVE THANKS

GIVE THANKS WITH A GRATEFUL HEART

GOD IS ALWAYS GOOD

The Psalms are a rich source of encouragement and inspiration to mankind. Generation after generation finds comfort in its poetry. It is one of the most quoted writings in the world and has inspired great music from composers and musicians of all types, from Beethoven to Bob Marley.

Some people treat the Psalms as merely a collection of inspirational phrases, as incantations to ward off evil. Others dismiss them as religious fables and nursery rhymes, but they are much more than these.

The Psalms express the inspired thoughts of Godly persons. Their words emerge from the rough and tumble of their lives, their moments of dark despair, their times of trouble and fear, their times of hunger and pain. In those dark places they discover an intimacy with their God, and a knowledge of Him, that escaped them in the more tranquil and placid pastures of their life.

The Psalmists' sometimes 'mix it up' . . . sometimes delicate in their words, sometimes boisterous and even cantankerous, sometimes brutal in their honesty, but always true to themselves, to their experiences and to their God.

The Psalms are not "politically correct" literature. They are not sanitized for polite company. The Psalms are radical and revolutionary. They cause us to confront our realities and circumstances as they are. But there is a theme of resistance and resilience that runs through the Psalms. A theme that says, the reality I see, is not the sum total of my reality. There is more, there is a game changer, someone has the "reset button" for my life, and that someone is Jehovah God.

It is in this context that I invite you to look at Psalm 107. It is about thanksgiving. It is about a God who is to be thanked for who he is and what he does. It is about a people who though undeserving, have experienced his goodness, his blessings and are returning to him with hearts overflowing with gratitude. The Psalmist is emphasizing to us that the focus of thanksgiving is God. God the giver and sustainer, not man the receiver and the object of his mercy.

You may be going through a storm, dark clouds may be hiding the sun, you may be weary and your heart may be fainting. You may even have convinced yourself that things are so bad, that there is no hope for tomorrow, and nothing to give thanks for today.

But I encourage you to read the Psalms, and discover, that in this your time of personal pain, is a Psalm waiting to emerge, your own song of thanksgiving. A Psalm to lift your faith, energize your spirit and inspire those around you, because things may be bad, but God is always good!

"O give thanks unto the Lord, for he is good; for his mercies endureth forever. . . Oh that men would praise the Lord for his goodness, and for his wonderful works to the children of men! - Psalm 107: 1&15 (KJV)

GIVE THANKS

Thanksgiving is an exercise that brings satisfaction both to the person giving thanks and to the person receiving it. It is an expression of appreciation and gratitude that enriches the human experience and tends to bring out the best in us.

When we give thanks, we are acknowledging that we have received something of value, something that means much to us, something that we appreciate. It is acknowledging that some act of generosity or thoughtfulness has made a difference to our lives and we want to show it.

When we take the time to give thanks, it gives us an opportunity to see how blessed we are, and we are able to recognize the many ways in which our lives have been enriched by the actions of others. When we receive thanks from others, we appreciate how blessed we are to be able to give, and how much our actions have enriched the lives of others.

Let us give thanks for the big things and little things in our lives. The milestones achieved, the victories won, the people we love and those who love us. The air we breathe and the ability to breathe in that air on our own. The beauty we see, the joy of simple things and the richness of the life that God gives each of us.

Let us be generous in expressing our gratitude to each other and to those we meet, as we take our journey through life. Let us take the time to show to those around us what we appreciate about them, and how much we appreciate them. Let us take the time to give thanks to God. He is the one who makes all things possible and without whom life would not exist.

"It is a good thing to give thanks unto the Lord, and to sing praises unto thy name, most High. To shewing forth thy loving kindness in the morning and thy faithfulness every night. Upon an instrument of ten strings and upon the psaltery: upon the harp with a solemn sound. For thou, Lord, hast made me glad through thy work: I will triumph in the works of thy hands." - Psalm 92:1-4 (KJV)

GIVE THANKS WITH A GRATEFUL HEART

As children, we were encouraged to express gratitude to others when we received a gift or favour. Thank you, was an expression that would come naturally from any well brought up child. As adults, we know that saying thanks is the polite way to acknowledge a good deed, and is one of the things that separates the "civilized" person from the "barbarian".

Giving thanks however, can become a routine. Something we do without even thinking. A mindless and sometimes meaningless act. Giving thanks can become just a transaction, as pretty as a plastic smile and just as insincere. It neither enriches the giver nor the recipient, robbing both of the opportunity to connect in any meaningful way.

But when we give thanks from a truly grateful heart, when it is not just the product of the lips, but a thoughtful response to an act of kindness, it adds a special quality to the exchange. This type of giving thanks is a gift in itself, it is the 'gift of gratitude.'

Giving the gift of gratitude requires us to acknowledge and appreciate the gift and the giver. To regard ourselves as being especially privileged to have received whatever it is that was given to us. To recognize that the giver parted with something of value in order to add value to us. To appreciate that the giver took the time to attend to our needs, possibly at the expense of attending to their own needs.

It requires that we dispense with the notion that we are entitled to certain things and that others are obliged to make us happy, or to keep us happy. It is to live with a sense of being privileged. . . privileged to live, privileged to move, privileged to be able to interact socially with others, privileged to enjoy the gifts of life, privileged to be created in the image of God and to be the recipients of His love.

The gift of gratitude is not an act, it is an attitude. It is a state of mind, a state of heart, a state of being. It has its origins in a loving God, who in the words of the Psalmist," daily loadeth us with benefits." A God who desires only the best for us and is constantly at work on our behalf. A God who tells us that all things work together for good to them that love Him.

David knew this God intimately. He had experienced his blessings. He had experienced his protection and his provision. He had also experienced His punishment and His pain. But David discovered and demonstrated the gift of gratitude. His writings overflow with appreciation for God's goodness. Even in what were obviously difficult times, his expressions of praise or pain, were laid on a bed of enduring gratitude to God.

Throughout the Psalms we hear him saying, "'O let us give thanks unto the Lord for He is good, because His mercies endureth forever." These passages are colourful and dramatic. They show his great confidence in God. His appreciation for God's blessings and the joy he finds in living close to God.

One cannot escape however, the context of conflict that is mixed-in with David's thanksgiving. One cannot ignore his calls for judgement upon his enemies, or the "warrior" in the writer. But through it all, David always ends up taking us to a special place, a place of gratitude.

Psalm 92, is a great example of the Psalmist, soaring to great heights of gratitude, in a stormy period of his life. It gives us words to lift us above the turbulence of today. To enjoy with gratitude, the presence of the God who occupies our todays, as well as our tomorrows. He starts with the value of thanksgiving, drops in some comments on his enemies and the wicked, and concludes with encouraging promises for the righteous.

He says: *"It is a good thing to give thanks unto the Lord, and to sing praises unto thy name, O most High: to show forth thy loving kindness in the morning, and thy faithfulness every night, upon an instrument of ten strings, and upon the psaltery; upon the harp with a solemn sound. For thou Lord, hast made me strong through thy work; I will triumph in the works of thy hands. . . Mine eyes shall also shall see my desire on mine enemies and mine ears shall hear the desire of the wicked that rise up against me. The righteous shall flourish like the palm tree: he shall grow like a cedar in Lebanon. Those that be planted in the house of the Lord shall flourish in the courts of our God. They shall bring forth fruit in old age; they shall be fat and flourishing; To show that the Lord is upright: he is my rock, and there is no unrighteousness in him." - Psalm 92: 1-3 & 12-15 (KJV)*

As I come to "journey's end" in this first series of the Pastor's Pen, I encourage you in your reflection, to give God thanks for the gifts and givers He has given you, and as you go along, to appreciate and affirm the people in your life that make you a better person, and your world a better place. Give thanks with a grateful heart.

I give thanks to God for the privilege He has given me to "journey" with you and to share my thoughts with you. May you truly be inspired and encouraged. My life is all the richer for sharing with you, and I pray that as we journey together as Christians, and as seekers after truth, that we remain mindful, that all that we are, all that we give and all that we receive, are by His power, for His glory.

"Let the word of Christ dwell in you richly as you teach and admonish one another with all wisdom, and as you sing psalms, hymns and spiritual songs with gratitude in your hearts to God. And whatever you do, whether in word or deed, do it all in the name of the Lord Jesus, giving thanks to God the Father through him."
Colossians 3:16-17

"They shall speak of the glory of Your kingdom, and talk of Your power, to make known to the sons of men His mighty acts, and the glorious majesty of His kingdom" - Psalm 145: 11-12

HOPE FELLOWSHIP PRESS
Inspiring the World with God's Words

VISION
To be a valuable, critical, viable and sustainable Christian Ministry through the provision of a dynamic range of Publishing Services and material, in both print and digital format, in service to the Hope Fellowship Church and wider Christian Community, and the world to "the Glory of God, by the Power of God"

MISSION
To promote and advance the understanding and embrace of God, through Christian Literature that inspire, encourage and promote a life of holiness as directed by the Bible – the living word of God

PROFILE

Hope Fellowship Press (HFP) is a dynamic and multi-faceted publisher of books, and a diverse range of other material, in print and digital format, designed to provide spiritual enrichment and practical help to people who are, or are desirous of becoming followers of Christ. HFP has also consciously broadened its publishing programme and service, to include the editorial, production, packaging, promotion, distribution and/or sale of select Christian material for the wider Christian Community.

Hope Fellowship Press was established in 2016, as a Publishing Ministry of Hope Fellowship Church, located in Kingston, Jamaica, dedicated to strengthening the Christian faith, and encourage all people to live for "the Glory of God, by the Power of God". Hope Fellowship Church, though grounded in the Holiness worship tradition, welcome and embrace all members of the Christian Faith.

OUR PRAYER

Father, we thank you for your guidance in establishing this Publishing Ministry, ***Hope Fellowship Press****, and we thank you for all whom you will send to join us, with their talents and gifts, to communicate through books and other resources, the power and glory of your name and the blessing of your great love for mankind. We pray that you may grow and prosper our Ministry and lead and guide us to glorify You in all that we do, and by so doing empower lives of service to you. In Jesus' name we pray all these things. Amen.*

www.ingramcontent.com/pod-product-compliance
Lightning Source LLC
Chambersburg PA
CBHW070141100426
42743CB00013B/2787